The Politics of Che Guevara

The Politics of Che Guevara

Theory and Practice

Samuel Farber

Haymarket Books
Chicago, Illinois

© 2016 Samuel Farber

First published in 2016 by
Haymarket Books
P.O. Box 180165
Chicago, IL 60618
773-583-7884
www.haymarketbooks.org
info@haymarketbooks.org

ISBN: 978-1-60846-601-6

Trade distribution:
In the US, Consortium Book Sales and Distribution, www.cbsd.com
In Canada, Publishers Group Canada, www.pgcbooks.ca
In the UK, Turnaround Publisher Services, www.turnaround-uk.com
All other countries, Publishers Group Worldwide, www.pgw.com

This book was published with the generous support of Lannan Foundation
and Wallace Action Fund.

Cover design by Samantha Farbman.

Printed in Canada by union labor.

Library of Congress Cataloging-in-Publication data is available.

10 9 8 7 6 5 4 3 2 1

Contents

Selected Chronology*

Major Events in Ernesto "Che" Guevara's Life and Cuban History, 1928–1967

June 14, 1928
Ernesto Guevara de la Serna is born in Rosario, Argentina, to Ernesto Guevara Lynch and Celia de la Serna.

August 1933–January 1934
Revolutionary overthrow of dictatorship of Gerardo Machado in Cuba. United States refuses to recognize nationalist government of Ramón Grau San Martín. Army strongman Fulgencio Batista rises to power with US support.

1934
Platt Amendment giving the United States legal power to intervene in Cuban affairs is officially overturned, but the United States retains a naval base in Guantánamo Bay. Reciprocal Trade Agreement between Cuba and the United States is signed, reinforcing Cuba's sugar monoculture and lack of industrial diversification.

1934–1940
Batista controls Cuba through puppet governments.

1940
New Cuban Constitution is enacted.

---

* Adapted in part from "Chronology of Ernesto Che Guevara," in Ernesto Che Guevara, *Reminiscences of the Cuban Revolutionary War* (Melbourne: Ocean Press, 2006), xiii–xxiii.

1940–1944
Batista rules Cuba as constitutional president.

1944–1952
Ramón Grau San Martín and Carlos Prío Socarrás rule Cuba in a generally democratic but corrupt fashion. Prío Socarrás is unable to finish his term.

January–July 1952
Ernesto Guevara travels through Latin America with his friend Alberto Granado.

March 10, 1952
Retired general Fulgencio Batista overthrows Prío's government through a military coup and constitutional government comes to an end.

Summer 1953
After graduating as a doctor in March, Ernesto Guevara travels again through Latin America. He visits Bolivia, shortly after the 1952 revolution.

July 26, 1953
Attack on Moncada Barracks by the Castro brothers and their followers fails, some are killed in combat, some are later assassinated by Batista's troops, and the remainder are jailed.

December 1953
Ernesto Guevara meets a group of Cuban survivors of the Moncada attack in San José, Costa Rica.

December 24, 1953
Ernesto Guevara arrives in Guatemala, then under the democratically elected reform government of Jacobo Árbenz.

January–June 1954
While in Guatemala, Che Guevara studies Marxism and becomes

involved in political activities, meeting another group of exiled Cuban revolutionaries.

August 1954
Troops backed by the CIA enter Guatemala City and begin killing Árbenz supporters.

September 21, 1954
Ernesto Guevara arrives in Mexico City after fleeing Guatemala.

May 15, 1955
Batista decrees political amnesty, and the Castro brothers, the rest of the Moncada attackers, and other political prisoners are released from prison.

July 1955
Ernesto Guevara meets Fidel Castro soon after the latter arrives in exile in Mexico City. Che immediately agrees to join the planned guerrilla expedition in Cuba. The Cubans nickname him "Che," an Argentine term of greeting.

December 2, 1956
The boat *Granma* lands in Oriente Province in Cuba, bringing Fidel Castro, Che Guevara as troop doctor, and eighty other anti-Batista fighters from Mexico.

July 21, 1957
Che Guevara is selected to lead the newly established second column (named "Column 4") of the Rebel Army and is promoted to the rank of major (the highest rank).

April 9, 1958
General strike against the Batista dictatorship fails.

May 3–5, 1958
Leaders of the Rebel Army and of the urban underground of the July 26th movement meet to discuss the defeat of the general strike at Altos

de Mompié. Che Guevara proposes the subordination of the urban struggle to guerrilla warfare in the countryside. The Rebel Army and the July 26th urban underground movement adopt Che's strategy.

December 28, 1958
Che Guevara's Column 8 initiates the battle of Santa Clara in central Cuba.

January 1, 1959
Batista flees Cuba.

January 8, 1959
Che Guevara is declared a Cuban citizen.

May 1959
The Agrarian Reform Law is enacted. Major growth of US state opposition to the Cuban government.

June 12–September 8, 1959
Che Guevara travels through Europe, Africa, and Asia as a representative of the Cuban government.

October 7, 1959
Che Guevara is designated head of the Department of Industry of the National Institute of Agrarian Reform.

November 1959
Tenth National Labor Congress convenes. Fidel Castro directly intervenes to press for "unity" slate with pro-Communist delegates.

November 25, 1959
Che Guevara is appointed president of the National Bank of Cuba.

March 1960
US government adopts systematic covert action plans to overthrow the Cuban government. Plans had been in preparation since late 1959.

May 1960

Fidel Castro achieves complete control of Cuban press and mass media. The Soviet Union and Cuba resume full diplomatic relations.

June–July 1960

US-owned oil companies refuse to process Soviet oil and are then expropriated by Cuban government. Eisenhower abrogates Cuban sugar quota.

August–October 1960

Large-scale expropriation of US-owned property in Cuba.

October 1960

Full-scale US economic blockade of Cuba begins. Large-scale expropriation of property owned by Cuban capitalists is undertaken.

1961

Formation of the Organizaciones Revolucionarias Integradas, uniting the three principal organizations—July 26th movement, Directorio Revolucionario, and Popular Socialist Party (Partido Socialista Popular [PSP], the old pro-Moscow Cuban Communists)—that fought against the Batista dictatorship as a first step toward the formation of the Cuban Communist Party.

January 3, 1961

Washington breaks diplomatic relations with Cuba.

February 23, 1961

The revolutionary government establishes the Ministry of Industry and appoints Che Guevara as its head. During his tenure as minister of industry, Guevara establishes the first civilian labor camp in Guanahacabibes in western Cuba.

April 15, 1961

The United States directs bombing of Cuban airfields.

April 16, 1961

Fidel Castro declares the "socialist" character of the revolution.

April 17–19, 1961

Bay of Pigs invasion of Cuba organized by the United States is defeated. Che Guevara is sent to command troops in western Pinar del Rio province in preparation for a possible US invasion of Cuba.

November 1961

Eleventh Congress of the Cuban Trade Union central organization. Unanimity replaces the controversy of the 1959 Tenth Congress. Old Stalinist labor leader Lázaro Peña elected secretary general.

October 1962

Cuban missile crisis; Che Guevara is assigned to lead forces in western Pinar del Rio province in preparation for an imminent US invasion.

February 24, 1965

Che Guevara addresses the Second Economic Seminar of the Organization of Afro-Asian Solidarity in Algiers and criticizes the Soviet bloc for complicity in the imperialist exploitation of the Third World.

March 14, 1965

Che Guevara returns to Cuba and shortly afterward disappears from public view.

April 1, 1965

Che Guevara delivers a farewell letter to Fidel Castro. He subsequently leaves the island on a Cuban-sponsored internationalist mission in the Congo, Africa, entering through Tanzania.

October 3, 1965

Fidel Castro publicly reads Che Guevara's letter of farewell at a meeting to announce the central committee of the newly formed Communist Party of Cuba.

November 21, 1965
Che Guevara leaves the Congo and begins writing up his account of the African mission, which he describes as a "failure."

December 1965
Fidel Castro arranges for Che Guevara to return to Cuba in secret. Che Guevara prepares for a Cuban-sponsored guerrilla expedition to Bolivia.

1966
Che Guevara completes notebooks, including material that will later be published as *Apuntes críticos a la economía política* (*Critical Notes on Political Economy*).

November 4, 1966
Che Guevara arrives in La Paz, Bolivia, in disguise.

November 7, 1966
Che Guevara and several others arrive at the farm on the Nacahuazú River where the guerrilla detachment will be based.

December 31, 1966
Che Guevara meets with Mario Monje, the secretary of the Bolivian Communist Party. There is disagreement over the leadership and perspectives for the planned guerrilla movement.

May 1967
US Special Forces arrive in Bolivia to train counterinsurgency troops of the Bolivian Army.

September 26, 1967
Che Guevara's guerrilla unit falls into a Bolivian Army ambush at Quebrada de Batán, near La Higuera.

October 8, 1967
The remaining seventeen guerrillas are trapped by army troops and conduct a desperate battle in the Quebrada del Yuro (El Yuro ra-

vine). Che Guevara is seriously wounded and captured.

October 9, 1967

Che Guevara and two other captured guerrillas are murdered by Bolivian soldiers following instructions from the Bolivian government and Washington.

Introduction

Che Guevara's
Political Relevance Today

Ernesto "Che" Guevara today has become a commercial T-shirt icon, but more importantly, he is an appealing symbol to legions of young rebels and revolutionaries all over the world. It is ironic that, politically, he has become less relevant in today's Cuba than he is in other countries around the world. Nevertheless, he continues to exercise a subtle but real influence on Cuba's political culture—not as a source of specific programmatic political or economic proposals, but as a cultural model of sacrifice and idealism. In that limited sense, the official slogan "*seremos como el Che*" (we shall be like Che), chanted regularly by Cuban schoolchildren, probably has a diffuse but significant influence over the popular imagination, even if most Cubans also think of Che as a failed quixotic figure.

•

Under Raúl Castro's leadership, the Cuban government has been striving, albeit with setbacks and contradictions, toward a Cuban version of the Sino-Vietnamese model, a form of state capitalism calling for the development of Cuban and especially foreign private enterprise while the state, under the exclusive control of the Communist Party, retains the commanding heights of the economy, a far cry from Guevara's proposed model of state control of the whole economy.

Che is not at all influential among the various wings of the Cuban opposition. Thus, for example, the liberal Cubans collaborating with Catholic reformists in what they hope will become a "loyal opposition" argue for ideas that run counter to Guevara's legacy, such as creating a government that promotes private enterprise, accompanied by liberal and democratic political reforms, which the Cuban one-party state is not likely to entertain given the risks this would pose to its control.[1] The nascent Cuban critical left, expressing its views on websites such as *Havanatimes.org* and *ObservatorioCritico.info*, and composed of people influenced by anarchist and/or social-democratic politics, is focusing its efforts on worker self-management and cooperatives as the road for economic democracy, an institutional arrangement that was explicitly rejected by Che Guevara.[2]

Che Guevara's politics have their greatest appeal outside of Cuba. It is true that the small political groups that follow Guevara's politics and ideology in toto have rarely attained any significance or influence, but important groups and movements that are not Guevaraist nevertheless claim to be influenced by Che beyond his mere image of the romantic and idealistic revolutionary. This is the case for people like Subcomandante Marcos (now renamed Subcomandante Galeano), the founding leader of the EZLN (Ejército Zapatista de Liberación Nacional) in Chiapas, Mexico, attracted by Che's call to take up arms against oppressive and corrupt governments. Even though Marcos rejected the notion of seizing political power, an idea central to Guevara's political ideology and strategy, he took up arms against an unjust system and cited Guevara's political ideas and practice as an inspiration. In that same spirit of insurgent rebellion, the 1968 Mexican student movement took over the Justo Sierra Auditorium at the UNAM (Universidad Nacional Autónoma de México, the Autonomous National University of Mexico) and renamed it the Che Guevara Auditorium.

In a broader sense, for many rebellious young people throughout the world, Che Guevara is seen as a key leader of the Cuban Revolution—one of the most important revolutions of the twentieth century—and the only one who coherently practiced what he preached. Even more appealing to many are Che's personal values: political honesty, egalitarianism, radicalism, and willingness to sacrifice for a cause, including his position of power in Cuba. To many of the contemporary rebels active in anticapitalist movements, Che is not only a radical, uncompromising opponent of capitalism, but—given his opposition to the traditional pro-Moscow Communist parties—also a revolutionary who shares their own ideals in pursuit of revolutionary and antibureaucratic politics. This is what makes Che's ideas and practices important, and this study relevant, in today's world.

This book analyzes the substantive political ideas and practices of Che Guevara from a standpoint that shares this anticapitalist, antibureaucratic sentiment. It does so, however, based on the belief that socialism and democracy are indispensable requisites to realize those aspirations. I was born and raised in Cuba and participated in the anti-Batista high school student movement of the 1950s, and have been involved in socialist politics for well over fifty years. My political roots are in the classical Marxist tradition that preceded Stalinism in the Soviet Union. Soviet Stalinism established the structural paradigm of a one-party state ruling over the whole economy, polity, and society—a paradigm that was later implemented in its multiple national variations by countries such as China, Vietnam, and Cuba. Central to my perspective is a view of socialist democracy in which institutions based on majority rule control the principal sources of economic, social, and political power at the local and national levels. To be a fully participatory democracy, socialism must be based on the self-mobilization and organization of the people, and the rule of the majority has to be complemented by minority rights and civil liberties.

I have written three books and numerous articles on Cuba based on this perspective. Che Guevara is a central part of the story of the Cuban Revolution, but his life and politics have international and theoretical repercussions that go beyond the Cuban story itself. In that sense, this study is closely related to another of my books, *Before Stalinism: The Rise and Fall of Soviet Democracy*, published in 1990.[3] In that book about the decline of the Russian Revolution, I discussed the degeneration of the democratic soviets that came to power with the triumph of the 1917 October Revolution. While clearly distinguishing Leninism in power from Stalinism, I nevertheless argued that, under the great pressures of the civil war and severe economic crisis, mainstream Bolshevism changed its political character, converting the necessity of repression under civil war conditions into a virtue, thus weakening the resistance to the subsequent emergence of Stalinism. That book focused on the issue of democracy and revolution, as does this study of Che Guevara's political thought and practice. Although of course the political background and historical conditions under which Guevara fought for his ideas were very different from those of the Russian Revolution, they also require us to consider the relationship between revolution and democracy. As will become evident in the rest of this study, while Guevara was an honest and dedicated revolutionary, he did not share Lenin's background in classical Marxism, which assumed the democratic heritage of the radical wing of the Enlightenment, but instead grew up with the political legacy of a Stalinized Marxism. Thus, his revolutionary perspectives were irremediably undemocratic, based on a conception of socialism from above rather than below, which raises serious questions about the social and political order he would have brought about had he been successful in his efforts to spark victorious revolutions in the Congo and Bolivia.

Che's Communism[4]

Che Guevara became a Communist in his mid-twenties. To Che, the state was the fulcrum of change and its takeover was the goal of the socialist revolution. But he was an idiosyncratic Communist: he did not join the Communist Party and eventually became highly critical of various features of the Soviet social and political system. He was an extreme voluntarist, holding views more closely resembling Mao's Chinese Communist politics than those of the Soviet Union. But even when he became more critical of the Soviet system after leaving the Cuban government, he upheld until the end of his life the monolithic Soviet view of socialism as a one-party state. Che was neither a libertarian nor a democrat in his theory or practice. His socialism/communism precluded any conception of autonomous workers and popular power, or of the political conditions necessary for the existence and survival of the institutions of popular and workers' control such as freedom of organization for groups such as workers, Blacks, and women and civil liberties such as freedom of speech and assembly. For Che, the essence of socialism consisted in the absolute elimination of competition and capitalist profit, and in having the state, led by the vanguard Communist Party, control the economic life of the country in its totality. His priority, in terms of the state's exclusive management of the economy, was to eliminate privilege and establish economic equality. His monolithic view of state socialism rejected not only the notion of workers' control and self-management, but of individual identity, interest, and self-determination (which should not be confused with individualism as the ideology and practice of the capitalist order). In his conception of economic equality and his insistence on an exclusive dedication to the goals of society, he implicitly accepted the old Tocquevillian dichotomy of equality versus individuality.

Che Guevara and the Road to Power

Che Guevara's views and practices regarding the road to power reiterate the perennial issue of the relationship between revolutionary means and ends. Che Guevara considered himself a Marxist and seriously studied the Marxist classics but was very selective of the aspects of Marxism he adopted as his own. Marx and Engels held that "the emancipation of the working classes must be conquered by the working classes themselves."[5] They assumed that as the working class became the majority of society, it would carry out its self-emancipation through a revolution in the interests of that majority. But, as we shall see, as early as when he was in the Sierra Maestra in 1958, Guevara in contrast became the principal proponent of the view that the guerrilla rebel army itself—and not the working class or, for that matter, the peasantry, except as supporting actors—would overthrow the Batista dictatorship and carry out the social revolution in Cuba. Che turned out to be right, in the practical sense of seizing power—although he greatly underestimated the major role played by the far more dangerous struggle of the urban revolutionaries in achieving Cuba's revolution of 1959.[6]

Although effective in overthrowing the old political and social system, Guevara's approach diverged from the classical Marxist politics of self-emancipation and socialist democracy. But it was entirely consistent with the establishment of a socialism from above, which initially enjoyed overwhelming support; it emphasized popular participation while excluding popular democratic control. Thus, the system established by Guevara and the other Cuban leaders on principle did not allow for the establishment of socialist democratic institutions and the political liberties and rights necessary for their fulfillment.

That Guevara's political and military methods worked under the social and political conditions that existed in the Cuba of the 1950s did not mean that they would work elsewhere. Che used the same fundamental approach in his guerrilla incursions in the Congo and especially in Bolivia without ever reassessing his assumptions regarding the socioeconomic and political conditions necessary for the success of guerrilla warfare. In the case of the Congo (while he later acknowledged the absence of conditions for a social or even an anti-imperialist revolution in the eastern part of that country), where he had led Cuban and Congolese soldiers, he nevertheless insisted, with extreme voluntarism, that the solution to those very real objective obstacles was the creation of a vanguard party. And in the case of Bolivia, he advised militant miners to abandon the mass struggle in the places where they lived and struggled and instead to join his faraway guerrilla army, which, in contrast with the democratic revolutionary traditions of the miners, was organized on a strictly military hierarchical basis and led mostly by people foreign to their class and country. In these two cases, Guevara's approach was neither effective nor self-emancipatory—and certainly not democratic.

Revolution, Socialism, and Democracy

The critical framework I use as the basis of this discussion of Che's political thought and practice favors revolution, which I see not as an inevitable explosion, but as a political reaction to changes in the real conditions that prevail in society. In this context, revolutionary violence is unfortunate, but necessary and inevitable in light of what oppressive ruling groups will do in order to preserve their power. There are, of course, critics of Che who claim that his resort to revolution and revolutionary violence itself is the cause of his "mistakes" or "failure." One of them, Jorge G. Castañeda, a prominent Mexican writer with deep roots in his country's political establishment (both he and his father were members of his country's cabinet at different times), criticizes Che's "eternal refusal of ambivalence." Castañeda laments the tendency of the 1960s generation to which he belonged to engage in "a wholesale rejection of life's contradictions" and to neglect the "very principles of contradictory feelings, of conflicting desires, of mutually incompatible goals" in an era that was "writ in black and white."[7] In his argument, Castañeda conflates the generally justifiable criticisms that he makes of guerrilla warfare as a revolutionary strategy and specific applications of it, as in the Congo and Bolivia with Marxist revolutionary politics and strategy as such. His clear implication is that reform, not revolution, is the only viable, sensible alternative in fighting for liberty and democracy.

This point of view is hardly unique to Castañeda. At least since the Russian Revolution, it has become accepted almost as political common sense that revolution and its violence are incompatible with democracy and liberty and that only parliamentary social reform can coexist with a democratic political order. In the mid-twentieth century, this perspective was not only maintained by prominent critics of Marxism such as the philosopher Karl Popper but at least implicitly by authentic socialist leaders such as Salvador Allende. As the democratically elected president of Chile, overthrown and killed in a military coup supported by the CIA, Allende sacrificed his life to remain faithful to that notion. That is why he refused to heed the call of his more militant supporters to arm the people to confront the armed forces' monopoly of violence and support for the capitalist status quo.

The relationship between revolution and democracy is a very important issue and a difficult one to disentangle. Nevertheless, I would assert that the following two points are vital: First, revolution does not automatically lead to dictatorship, totalitarianism, or democracy. It is true that any situation of active armed conflict—revolutionary or otherwise—inevitably involves the curtailment of the democratic process and of civil liberties. But what happens after the armed conflict has ceased and the revolutionary power is stabilized, although economic crisis may act as a restraining and limiting force, depends to an important extent on the politics of the revolutionary leaders in determining whether the encroachment on democracy and liberties during the armed conflict are to be made permanent, thus converting what originally might have been a necessity into a virtue. Second, a social revolution does not necessarily lead to the collective punishment of social groups or categories of people—whether based on race, class, religion, or ethnicity—in contrast with the necessary punishment of individuals or specific groups who engage in armed actions against the revolutionary government. For example, in the aftermath of the 1917 Bolshevik revolution, universal suffrage—an enormous achievement of the democratic struggles that arose in the wake of epoch-making movements such as the French Revolution and the Chartist movement in Britain—was curtailed by the provisions contained in chapters 5 and 13 of the Soviet Constitution promulgated in July 1918. These chapters established, respectively, the obligation of all citizens to work and confined the franchise to those who earned their living by production or socially useful labor, soldiers, and disabled persons, and specifically excluded persons who employed hired labor, rentiers, private traders, monks and priests, and officials and agents of the former police. In her famous pamphlet on the Russian Revolution, Rosa Luxemburg criticized these exclusions, arguing that the Russian economy was in no condition to offer gainful employment to all who requested it, thereby disenfranchising those who might have been involuntarily unemployed.[8] While this is a legitimate point, Luxemburg missed the central issue behind the legislation. The aim of the Bolshevik government was not the disenfranchisement of the idle or the unemployed in general, but to punish every member of the bourgeoisie and allied strata, such as the church, even if they requested state employment after having lost their business, factories, and churches. This notion of collective punishment gained traction at the same time that Lenin explicitly indicated that he regarded these exclusions not as matters of general principle regarding the general nature of the dictatorship of the proletariat but as the result of specific Russian conditions, that is, the extreme resistance offered by bourgeois and petty bourgeois circles to the October Revolution and to the radical and initially democratic changes introduced by it.[9] Nevertheless, the practice of collective punishment originally applied to the bourgeoisie and its allied strata had dire legal and political consequences for all classes and groups in Soviet Russia. Thus, it was that same notion of collective punishment that was used to repress and kill peasants in the Tambov region whether or not they had personally aided or participated in the so-called green peasant rebellions in 1920–21.[10] Luxemburg made a comment relevant to this point when she remarked that the suffrage law in Russia "involves a deprivation of rights not as a concrete measure for a concrete purpose but as a general rule of long-standing effect," though she did not make this the central element of her critique.[11]

The question of disenfranchisement is also related to the issue of the degree to which socialist democratic representation should be workplace based. This is a matter in which the classical Marxist tradition has been less than fully clear, since its indispensable critique of the vices of liberal capitalist parliamentary democracy does not settle the question of whether workplace representation would be sufficient by itself to represent all sectors of the population.[12] In any case, a workplace- and class-centered socialist democracy should not mean the disenfranchisement and denial of rights to various types of workers, such as the self-employed, and to individual members of the defeated classes who are willing to work and live peacefully in the new system. The working-class nature of the new socialist system is most of all established by the actual political leadership of the working class and its allies and by a political system structured in such a way as to favor the collective workplace instead of the isolated individual citizen. It should not mean a repudiation of the principles of universal suffrage and legal rights on behalf of which so much of the blood of the oppressed has been shed.

Che Guevara and Revolutionary Politics

One of the important features of Che Guevara's political thought and activism was his disregard for the specific political contexts as crucial guides for political action. His exclusive focus on making the revolution and on the tactics of the armed struggle led him, by the mid-1960s, to the conclusion that practically all the countries in Latin America were ready to take up arms in their rural hinterlands, ignoring the widely differing political and socioeconomic conditions prevailing throughout the continent. This strategic and tactical blindness came in part from his reaction to the electoralist tendencies and politicking prevalent among the old pro-Moscow Communist parties of his time. It is very illustrative that when Che Guevara met Mario Monje, the leader of the pro-Moscow Bolivian Communist Party, on December 31, 1966, to ask him to join the guerrilla foco that he had just established in the Bolivian hinterland, Monje responded, "In your head there is a machine gun, in mine there is politics."[13] For Monje and his party, the road to power might have formally involved, as for all the Communist parties, a general uprising, street mobilizations, and the militancy of the miners and

the unions. But their opportunistic practice of making pacts with corrupt parties and leaders was an entirely different matter, as was the case
with the old pro-Moscow Cuban Communists in the struggle against
the Batista dictatorship.[14]

There is, however, an alternative perspective to Che's revolutionary
voluntarism and to the Latin American Communist parties' electoralism
for its own sake and opportunism. It is a perspective that posits revolutionary politics as requiring strategic and tactical thinking and action
in order to advance the revolutionary process. In that sense, politics
is an imperative forced on the revolutionaries by stark political reality,
which includes what the ruling class and its allies will do to prevent any
changes that harm their interests. Political reality presents a great number of difficulties and options that continually pose anew the perennial
question of what is to be done—as well as the political goals and the
strategy and tactics best suited to attain them. As movements develop, in
addition to government surveillance, provocations, and repression, they
inevitably face the lies and propaganda of the rulers to weaken, divide,
and confuse them. The best responses to these challenges are often far
from obvious and require strategic and tactical tasks that help mobilize
and make people conscious of the nature of the enemy and its tactics.
Contrary to the Cuban revolutionary government's dictum that the
duty of the revolutionary is to make the revolution, most of the life of
a revolutionary is actually spent in the often dangerous task of fighting
political battles to advance the goals and interests of the working class
and the popular sectors and, in that process, to prepare for the revolution and the revolutionary situations that may make them possible. As
V. I. Lenin, the Bolshevik leader, famously put it:

> To the Marxist it is indisputable that a revolution is impossible without a
> revolutionary situation; furthermore, it is not every revolutionary situa-
> tion that leads to revolution. What, generally speaking, are the symptoms
> of a revolutionary situation? We shall certainly not be mistaken if we
> indicate the following three major symptoms: (1) when it is impossible
> for the ruling classes to maintain their rule without any change; when
> there is a crisis, in one form or another, among the "upper classes," a
> crisis in the policy of the ruling class, leading to a fissure through which
> the discontent and indignation of the oppressed classes burst forth. For
> a revolution to take place, it is usually insufficient for "the lower classes
> not to want" to live in the old way; it is also necessary that "the upper

classes should be unable" to live in the old way; (2) when the suffering and want of the oppressed classes have grown more acute than usual; (3) when, as a consequence of the above causes, there is considerable increase in the activity of the masses, who uncomplainingly allow themselves to be robbed in "peace time," but in turbulent times, are drawn both by all the circumstances of the crisis and by the "upper classes" themselves into independent historical action.[15]

Against the German social-democratic leader Karl Kautsky's passive and mechanical belief that socialist parties do not plan for revolution but that revolutions occur by themselves when objective conditions give rise to them, Lenin was a fervent proponent of the notion that a revolutionary party that seriously contended for power had to be ready, in a political and military sense, to lead revolutionary movements to the seizure of power, which required detailed attention to the specific political situation to determine the appropriate moment to do so. Otherwise, Lenin noted, things would not change and reaction would very likely set in. This is exactly what has happened in many cases—for example, during General Augusto Pinochet's coup in Santiago, Chile, on September 11, 1973, President Allende's commitment to parliamentarism facilitated the demise of his constitutional government.

Guevara, however, ignored the whole problematic of the "revolutionary situation," characteristically arguing, even in his original and relatively more cautious 1960 treatise on guerrilla warfare, that "it is not necessary to wait until all conditions for making revolution exist, the insurrection can create them."[16] Seven years later, Guevara became so isolated that it was possible for the Bolivian Army, working with the CIA, to murder him in cold blood in the Bolivian jungle. The utter failure of his guerrilla venture was hardly surprising given the absence of a revolutionary situation and a mistaken strategic orientation to the peasantry in an isolated and thinly populated part of the country, which failed to obtain any support from either the Bolivian peasantry or its working class.

Nature of This Study

The purpose of this project is to present a political portrait focused on Guevara's thought and practical political record. My aim is to understand his politics and the varying situations in which he acted, and in the process help to dispel many of the common myths about Che. I have drawn on a variety of sources, especially on my previous work on Cuba and the Cuban Revolution. However, two of my most fruitful sources are works by Guevara that were not intended for publication but emerged between thirty and forty years later, when changing political conditions, including the demise of the Soviet Union, convinced the Cuban government that it was no longer necessary to keep them under lock and key. These are *The African Dream: The Diaries of the Revolutionary War in the Congo*, published by Grove Press in 2001, which originally appeared in Spanish in 1999 under the title *Pasajes de la guerra revolucionaria: Congo*, and Guevara's notebooks, written in 1965 and 1966, published by Ocean Press (based in Australia) and the Cuban Centro de Estudios Che Guevara in 2006, under the title *Apuntes críticos a la economía política*. As in the case of the *Apuntes*, all translations from Spanish are my own, unless stated otherwise.

This book is divided into four main chapters, in addition to this introduction and the conclusion. Chapter 1 addresses Che Guevara's political upbringing in Argentina and how certain values and beliefs of his youth influenced his political theory and practice after he became an independent Communist in Guatemala in 1954. Chapter 2 is primarily focused on Guevara's political perspectives on revolutionary agency as he expressed them in his theory and practice of guerrilla warfare in Cuba, the Congo, and Bolivia. Chapter 3 addresses Guevara's record as a political leader and administrator in Cuba after the victory of the revolution, with special attention to the issue of democracy in a socialist society, and includes a detailed critique of his principal theoretical work, the pamphlet *Socialism and Man in Cuba*. Chapter 4 discusses in detail Guevara's views on political economy and the debate that took place among various groupings inside the Cuban government (and among some foreigners) concerning such topics as methods of economic planning, moral and material incentives, and the applicability of the law of value to socialist society. In my conclusion, I draw together some of the major themes in my analysis of Guevara's politics and restate the need for a political process that brings together the politics of revolution, socialism, and democracy.

Chapter One

The Bohemian Origins of Che Guevara's Politics

Guevara's Family Background and Youth

When Ernesto Guevara was born, in 1928, Argentina was the most economically developed country in Latin America. Right before World War I, Argentina resembled, in terms of its wealth, Australia, Canada, or New Zealand more than it resembled other Latin American countries. In 1913, its per capita income was the thirteenth largest in the world, slightly higher than France's.[1] The southern cone country had a powerful bourgeoisie that, in conjunction with the hierarchy of the influential Catholic Church and the powerful top army and navy brass, constituted an authentic Argentinian oligarchy. Both of Guevara's parents, Ernesto Guevara Lynch and Celia de la Serna, had high-society backgrounds. While Guevara senior was a spendthrift (as well as a bad businessman) and his family was often broke and experienced a certain degree of downward mobility, it still belonged to the "right" social class and retained the innate confidence of those born into affluence that things would turn out all right in the end.[2]

Che's architect father and his wife were cultured people. Celia in particular showed a strong affinity for French culture.[3] They were politically progressive people who closely followed and were strongly identified

1

with the fate of the Spanish Republic at a time when Argentina was witnessing the emergence of a nationalist, Catholic, and virtually fascist right that embraced anti-Semitism, racism, eugenics, and Nazism and that sided with right-wing general Francisco Franco in the Spanish Civil War (1936–39).[4] Later, they supported the Allied cause in World War II, and when the movement supporting Juan and Evita Perón developed shortly afterward, in the mid-1940s, a political phenomenon that disoriented much of the left and deprived it of popular support, they openly and unambiguously opposed it.[5]

The most distinctive characteristic of Che Guevara's parents, and of his mother Celia in particular, was not their relative downward mobility or their progressive politics but their incipient bohemianism.[6] This was a lifestyle whose adherents attempted to free themselves from many of the predominant cultural values, norms, and prejudices of the bourgeois world and at least implicitly posed a cultural critique of the conventions that governed that world.[7] Thus, Ernestito, or Teté (Che's childhood nicknames), was conceived out of wedlock, an unusual circumstance for upper-class Argentinians in the 1920s, in contravention to a number of social and religious taboos involving the preservation of a woman's virginity until marriage.[8] Contrary to the prevailing bourgeois norms regarding the proper appearance and administration of a respectable home, the Guevara household was disordered, even chaotic. Dedicated to the cult of creativity, Celia would bring home all kinds of colorful people from a wide variety of social backgrounds: from itinerant painters who worked as bootblacks to wandering foreign poets and university professors who stayed for any length of time, from a week to a month. In the process, Celia became estranged from her husband. Although they continued to live in the same house, they led increasingly separate lives.[9] Celia also encouraged her children to lead completely unstructured and disordered lives and to develop friendships with children of all social classes, who were welcome to play and eat in the Guevara household.[10] The Guevaras even stopped attending church in their regular parish after the priest berated Celia for the insufficiently modest dress she had worn to Mass.[11] They also requested of the schools that their children attended that they be exempted from religious classes.[12] Celia set several "firsts" for women in her socially conservative circles with such activities as driving a car and wearing trousers.[13] None of this, however, stopped

Celia and Ernesto Sr. from continuing to be well received in upper-class circles because of their cool elegance and indisputable pedigree, even if they were criticized behind their backs.

Ernesto Jr. grew up suffering from asthma and was forced to spend a lot of time in bed. He became an inveterate reader, especially of authors of adventure and science fiction, including the French authors Alexander Dumas and Jules Verne and the Italian writer Emilio Salgari, that for many decades were favored by young Latin American readers. Young Ernesto developed a strongly competitive personality and engaged in attention-getting exploits such as drinking ink out of a bottle and playing *torero* with an irascible ram.[14] His infrequent bathing, which may have been related to his asthma, and his parents' bohemianism may explain his adoption of a messy and slovenly appearance, which led his friends to call him "*el chancho*" or "the pig," a nickname that infuriated his father, who saw it as a slight to the family's honor.[15] Ernesto Jr. liked to shock people. In addition to his deliberately shabby appearance (he used to boast of not having washed his shirt in twenty-five weeks),[16] he was contemptuous of formality and demonstrated a confrontational sense of humor and combative intellect that would lead him to say outrageous things and scandalize people around him.[17] His contrarian style, however, did not extend to the gender norms of his time. Like his father and so many of his male contemporaries, he exhibited an ingrained "machismo" and a profound aversion to homosexuality.[18]

Yet, although the future Che shared the antifascist and progressive political inclinations of his family, he resisted getting involved in organized political activity in his teens and early twenties even though he had several friends and acquaintances who were members of the Federación Juvenil Comunista or Communist Youth.[19] However, his strong antifascist sentiments led him to stand up in class to a notoriously pro-Nazi history professor and to physically defend Raúl Melivosky, a Jewish student, from the bullying and physical threats of a fascist student group.[20] He also became attracted to the life and thought of Mahatma Gandhi, the father of Indian independence.[21] It is not difficult to understand Ernesto's affinity with Gandhi's thought. Aside from his opposition to British imperialism, Gandhi was at ease associating with people whom the ruling groups considered socially inferior, a trait that must have strongly resonated with the egalitarianism Guevara had acquired from his mother and that he so vigorously upheld until his death. He also shared with the Indian leader a profoundly ascetic disdain for material comforts (although in Guevara's case that might have derived from a bohemian critique of bourgeois materialism) and an opposition to injustice that was more moral than explicitly political.[22]

Politics was not a topic of conversation for the young Guevara in those days, and on the few occasions he did talk about politics, he tended to make radical and dramatic sounding pronouncements. He refused to join a street demonstration, claiming, "I will go if they give me a revolver, [since] without arms it is all a futile gesture, and I don't want to go just to be beaten up."[23] The young Guevara's reluctance to get involved in actual, organized political activity might be linked to the dominance that Peronismo had achieved in Argentine politics, including street politics, after the mid-1940s. Peronismo was an authoritarian and politically ambiguous movement that drew the support of the great majority of the Argentinian population, especially the working class, because of the material advantages and respect they gained as a consequence of the Perón government's policies. This placed the left in a very tough position of neither ignoring working-class and popular sentiments nor joining Perón and becoming apologists for his regime. Guevara's parents were firmly anti-Peronista, but Ernesto Jr., who sympathized with their general progressive politics, refused to take sides for or against Peronism, perhaps as a negative reaction to the pronounced class prejudices of the many middle- and upper-class anti-Peronistas that his family's social milieu represented.[24] He even seemed to have remained largely indifferent to what was the most important political event he had witnessed until then: the demonstrations of October 17, 1945, when the working class of Buenos Aires came out en masse to rescue Perón from prison and literally carried him to the presidency of Argentina.[25] It is likely that Guevara's abstention was a response to a very difficult political juncture for the left, which he, as a progressive bohemian, had no inclination to address.[26] But it was precisely this lack of involvement that prevented him from developing a sense for the portent of political events, which may help to explain the political tone-deafness—the frequent inability to understand specific political situations—he was to exhibit in the future. This stands in sharp contrast to Fidel Castro's ability to immediately intuit the nature and direction of the political conjuncture and develop a tactical response to it.

Nevertheless, Guevara's future political evolution must have drawn on the considerable political reading of his bohemian, pre-activist youth. As his biographer Jon Lee Anderson described it, Guevara had read in his early youth Benito Mussolini on fascism, Josef Stalin on Marxism, Alfredo Palacios (the Argentine socialist leader) on justice, Emile Zola on Christianity, Jack London on social class, some speeches of Lenin, *The Communist Manifesto*, and parts of *Capital*. He also filled several pages of his journal with a brief biography of Marx, culled from R. P. Ducatillon's *Marxism and Christianity*.[27]

Guevara's Travels and Political Evolution

It is only after he left Argentina and began his extensive travels through Latin America that Guevara gradually began to move toward political activism. Although he still described himself as a "100% adventurer" when he wrote to his mother in 1953 that he had decided to travel to Guatemala, there was a degree of sympathy and respect for left politics—specifically for Communism and its activists—that had been growing in him.[28] He admiringly described in his diary a rank-and-file Communist he met in his travels: "The communism gnawing at his entrails was no more than a longing for something better, a protest against persistent hunger transformed for a love for this strange doctrine, whose essence he could never grasp but whose translation 'bread for the poor' has something which he understood and more importantly filled him with hope."[29] Guevara's admiration for the Guatemalan Communists grew especially after the CIA-backed overthrow of the democratically elected government of Jacobo Árbenz in 1954. He took a clear position in support of the Guatemalan government and within it, with the PGT (Partido Guatemalteco del Trabajo), the Communist Party. He saw that party as the only political grouping that joined the government in order to comply with a program in which personal interests did not count, in frank contrast with the other groups and parties, which he saw as a veritable snakepit.[30] However, he was still reluctant to join the Communist Party because he disliked its "iron discipline" and also because he had plans to travel to Europe.[31]

Guevara's increasing attraction to Communism—and his eventual political engagement with the Cuban exiles in Mexico—was stimulated by the heartless poverty and oppression that he witnessed during his trip through Latin America. It was much worse than anything he had seen in his native country. He also came to associate the injustice of the lives of the people he had met through his journeys with the neocolonial exploitation suffered at the hands of US imperialism.[32] His attraction to Communism was reinforced by the extremely bad impression that representative figures of other tendencies of the broad Latin American left made on him. On one occasion he observed the employees of Ñuflo Chávez, the minister of peasant affairs of the MNR (Movimiento Nacionalista Revolucionário, the Nationalist Revolutionary Movement), the revolutionary government of Bolivia, disinfect with DDT the peasants waiting to see him. When Guevara and a friend complained to the minister about this degrading practice, the official justified his order as unfortunate but necessary, noting that the Indians were not familiar with the use of soap and that it would take years to change their cleaning habits. Shocked, Guevara concluded in his diary: "This revolution will fail unless it succeeds in breaking through the Indians' spiritual isolation, touching them to the core, shaking to their very bones, giving them back their stature as human beings. Otherwise, what good is it?"[33]

Guevara also had the opportunity to meet the Dominican Juan Bosch, a well-known opponent of Rafael Trujillo's dictatorship (1930–1961), and the Venezuelan Rómulo Betancourt, a leading figure of Latin American social democracy, when they were both exiled in Costa Rica. His appraisal of Betancourt was very negative: "He gives me the impression of being a politician with some firm social ideas in his head, but the rest are fluttery and twistable in the direction of the best advantages. In principle he's on the side of the United States. He went along with the [1948] Rio [Inter-American Defense] Pact and dedicated himself to speaking horrors of the Communists."[34] Juan Bosch came off better than Betancourt, but Guevara found Costa Rican Communist leader Manuel Mora Valverde's and his analysis of Costa Rican recent history and President José Figueres's pro-US policies more impressive.[35]

As Guevara traveled and drew closer to Communism, he already had a general political framework that gave meaning to his experiences. In addition to the particular influence of his parents, he grew up with certain "domain assumptions" that characterized the political culture of the broad progressive left in Latin America.[36] These included a deeply felt political and economic anti-imperialism articulated by a wide array of influential figures, from the Cuban Communist Julio Antonio Mella (1903–1929) and the Peruvian Communist pioneer José Carlos Mariátegui (1894–1930) to the Peruvian reformer Víctor Raúl Haya de la Torre (1895–1979) and the sui generis nationalism of the Argentinians Juan Perón (1895–1974) and Evita Perón (1919–1952). On the cultural front, this economic and political anti-imperialism became embodied in the classic essay *Ariel* by the Uruguayan writer José Enrique Rodó, which portrayed a utilitarian and materialistic United States that stood in opposition to the spiritual values that supposedly defined the essence of Latin America.

Another widespread assumption of the broad progressive left of Guevara's time combined a generalized distrust of governments with faith in the state as the guarantor of the collective good and the agent through which society could be effectively changed. This sentiment was accompanied among some sections of the broad left with a disdain for "bourgeois democracy." This position was based on the notion that individual political rights were somehow tainted by their association with the "formal democracy" preserving property established by bourgeois revolutions, such as the French Revolution.[37] Even more influential was the romantic and quixotic notion of honor and self-sacrifice in pursuit of righting wrongs. This Don Quixote/Jean Valjean syndrome emphasized sympathy and aid to victims, rather than the oppressed organizing themselves to reclaim their rights and gain power.

Guevara Meets the Cuban Exiles

In March 1952, Fulgencio Batista successfully carried out a military coup d'etat that brought him back to power after eight years of a constitutional and liberal democratic but very corrupt political regime in Cuba. However, Batista's government had a very limited social base and little support beyond the armed forces. In comparison to Perón's Argentina, it was much easier for Cuba's democratic and popular forces to define themselves in opposition to the regime.

By the 1950s, Cuba had the fourth-highest per capita income in Latin America, after Venezuela, Uruguay, and Argentina.[38] Even according to a broader set of indicators of general economic development, Cuba still ranked fourth in Latin America.[39] The island comprised a small territory, approximately the size of Pennsylvania, with a little less than six million people, and a much smaller territory and population than Argentina. But it was much more racially diverse, with Blacks and "mixed-race" people (called *mulattoes* in Cuba) jointly constituting, at the time, a little more than a fourth of the population.

While Cuba's bourgeoisie held substantial economic power, unlike Argentina, it was politically and culturally weak, partly because of its greater political and economic dependence on US imperialism and a widespread cultural imitation of the North American way of life. Cuban Catholicism was religiously and culturally weak in part because of its white, middle-class, and urban character and in part because of the important influence of African traditional religions and cultural practices that the Catholic hierarchy rejected as pagan, often with a tinge of racism. By the 1950s, the traditional Cuban right wing was much weaker in Cuba than in Argentina and was particularly concentrated in that part of the considerable Spanish immigrant population that had supported Franco in the Spanish Civil War. Ever since the frustrated 1933 revolution, the Cuban Army was led by former noncommissioned officers of plebeian background, such as Fulgencio Batista, who had replaced the older officer corps closely tied to the Cuban upper classes. While there was certainly a Cuban upper class, one cannot speak of a Cuban oligarchy in the same way as in Argentina. The absence of an oligarchy, properly speaking, the cultural weight of a disproportionately proletarian and poor Black and mixed-race population, and the influence of various aspects of "the American way of life" considerably weakened bourgeois hegemony over the values and culture of Cuban society of that period. While bohemianism has generally been a social phenomenon typical of the class systems and capitalist economic development prevalent in Europe and North America, the kind of anti-bourgeois cultural rebellion expressed by Che Guevara and his family would have been less likely to occur in the context of the much weaker bourgeois cultural hegemony in Cuba.[40]

The Cuban rebels that Guevara initially met in Guatemala (Antonio "Ñico" López, Mario Dalmau, Darío López, and Armando Arencibia) and the much larger group of Cuban rebels he met in Mexico later on were not at all bohemians, or sociocultural rebels like Guevara, but intensely political rebels.[41] They were "adventurers" like Guevara, but in a strictly political sense. For the most part, however, their political rebellion was not founded on any sort of Marxism, including that of the Cuban Communists, but on the late-nineteenth-century political thought of Cuban founding father José Martí, and on a militant "déclassé" political culture with a much thinner foundation of social theory than Guevara's. Moreover, the Cubans were more provincial, and far more culturally and politically nationalist, than Che Guevara. Fidel Castro was an intellectually curious and well-read man and could be considered an intellectual, but he was, above all, a man of action and, unlike Guevara, a quintessential revolutionary politician. The other Cubans associated with Fidel were generally not intellectuals. For example, their mastery of foreign languages was generally well below Che's command of French. But their intellectually unsophisticated passion made a big impression on Che. As he put it: "When I heard the Cubans make grandiloquent affirmations with absolute serenity I felt small. I can make a speech ten times more objectively. . . . I can read it better and convince an audience that I am saying something that is right, but I don't convince myself, and the Cubans do. Ñico [López] left his soul in the microphone, and for that reason he enthused even a skeptic such as myself."[42]

It was only after having met Fidel Castro and the members of the *Granma*[43] expedition to Cuba that Che met the pro-Moscow Cuban Communists. While they tended to be more theoretically developed than Fidel Castro's close associates, with a rigid and dogmatic adherence to the Stalinist version of "Marxism," they were no more likely than the Fidelistas to be inclined to a bohemian outlook and lifestyle. Instead, Cuban Communist intellectuals saw themselves as the defenders of "high culture," particularly in its Cuban version, against the vulgarity of the Cuban "nouveau riche" bourgeoisie. It was no accident that when the island's Communists founded the cultural organization Nuestro Tiempo (Our Time) in March 1951 (a year before Batista's coup), their initial interest was to disseminate and develop a public for classical and Cuban concert music, infrequently heard on Cuban radio and its nascent television stations. When Nuestro Tiempo also branched out to other cultural areas it did so based on a predilection for realism, undoubtedly influenced by Soviet socialist realism, which rejected works "with any type of evasion like surrealism or any other subjective form."[44] This specifically meant that in the fifties Nuestro Tiempo expressed a great deal of interest in the Italian neorealist cinema, which it saw as a contemporary embodiment of the realist tradition,[45] while frequently criticizing the "cosmopolitanism" that affected, in its view, such diverse artistic expressions as Hollywood movies and Cuban popular music.[46] It is ironic that Che Guevara, who for several years was an important and close political ally of the Cuban Communists, had nevertheless been influenced by Freud's psychology and Sartre's philosophical existentialism, was averse to socialist realism, and led a bohemian lifestyle. He was thus closer in certain respects to the avant garde circles in Western Europe and the imperialist United States than to either Cuban Stalinists or Fidelistas.[47] Nevertheless, while the Cuban Communists were politically less militant than the Fidelistas and other revolutionary groups, they were the most significant, socially radical political tendency in the Cuba of the 1950s. Their social radicalism, however, was based on a class and social analysis of politics that led them to a "socialist" outlook of Cuban society as a whole and not merely its political system.

Most of the Cuban rebels around Fidel Castro in Mexico who would later become the top leadership of the guerrilla army in the Sierra Maestra were "declassed," in the sense that they were detached from the organizational life of the Cuban working, middle, and upper classes.[48] However, they were not alienated from many of the conventions and cultural norms that guided the daily life of most of Cuban society, particularly those of its middle classes. The cultural difference between Che Guevara and many of the Cubans with whom he associated in Mexico occasionally created friction. When Melba Hernández, a mixed-raced lawyer who was a veteran of the Moncada attack and former political prisoner, arrived in Mexico, Che, who at this time had no substantial revolutionary merits to his credit, bluntly told her that she could not possibly be a revolutionary with so much jewelry on, declaring that "real revolutionaries adorn themselves on the inside, not on the surface." It is unlikely that Hernández had ever come across that point of view among Cuban revolutionaries, whether Communist or not. Eventually, however, she decided that Che was right and began to wear less jewelry.[49]

According to Hilda Gadea, a fellow exile from Peru who married Che in Mexico, Guevara used to be amused by the Cubans' mania for personal cleanliness, including their showering and changing clothes after they finished their daily tasks. "That's fine," Che said, "but what will they do in the hills? I doubt we'll ever be able to take a bath or change clothes. The most we do is save enough soap to wash plates and eating utensils so we won't get sick."[50] Events and developments after the victory of the 1959 Cuban Revolution showed that Guevara's judgments went beyond a realistic assessment of the material limitations of guerrilla warfare. When serious shortages of consumer goods began to occur in Cuba in the early 1960s, Che Guevara spoke critically about the comforts that Cubans had surrounded themselves with in the cities, and attributed them to the way in which imperialism had accustomed people. Thus, Guevara ignored how the relative economic development of the country and the working-class and popular struggles in the prerevolutionary era had improved the standard of living of Cuba's popular classes.[51] He argued that countries such as Cuba should invest completely in production for economic development, and that because Cuba was at war, the revolutionary government first had to ensure people had food. He regarded soap and similar goods as inessential.[52] Later, after the failure of the grandiose plans for economic growth that Guevara as minister of industry and other revolutionary leaders articulated, these general attitudes came to be shared by the entire Cuban government leadership and were soon consecrated in the Cuban revolutionary ideology as hostility to the "consumer society" of the economically developed world. However, nothing in the prerevolutionary ideology of what could have been called the Cuban left, whether Communist or not, had pointed in this direction, whereas Guevara's bohemian asceticism long predated his involvement with Cuba. His was a principled anticonsumerism. The Cuban leadership's was not: they did not necessarily apply it to their personal lives, as Guevara did, and instead used anticonsumerism to ideologically justify the results of their rule and help preserve it.

Some Conclusions

Many of the ideas and actions that characterized Che Guevara's political life are traceable to his personal history of growing up in a privileged milieu in the prosperous Argentina of the first half of the twentieth century. Prominent among these were his emphasis on egalitarianism and opposition to privilege; the advocacy of individual sacrifice for the sake of collective goals conceived in distinctive ascetic terms; a profound voluntarism—the idea that human will and consciousness can by itself over-come any objective, material obstacles; and a political tone-deafness that failed to recognize the specificity of political situations and conjunctures.

Although Che's bohemian asceticism was transformed when he be-came a fully dedicated political activist, he did not leave it behind. Thus, for example, at a meeting of the top managers of his Cuban Ministry of Industry in 1964, Guevara reflected on the difference between Cuba, where a television set that did not work was a problem, and Vietnam, where they were building socialism and there was no television at all. According to Guevara, the development of consciousness allows for the substitution of what he considered secondary comforts that at a certain point had become part of the life of the individual but that expresses a need that the overall education of society can eliminate.[53] Thus, Guevara was not merely suggesting that under certain conditions of political and economic crisis (as those Cuba was suffering in the sixties) people had to resign themselves to not having access to certain consumer goods. He went far beyond that to argue a much deeper political and even philo-sophical perspective, namely, that people should be educated into not wanting these goods at all by reverting to a previous period when those needs did not yet exist. Needless to add, it would be Guevara and the other revolutionary leaders who would be imposing the reduction of needs and options and therefore the goods that people should be "ed-ucated" not to desire. It is this asceticism that helps to explain his prin-cipled and enduring egalitarianism and (as will become evident in later chapters) his views and policies, after the revolutionary victory regarding popular consumption, his emphasis on moral incentives, and his concep-tion of socialism in his main work *Socialism and Man in Cuba*.

While it could be argued that Fidel Castro was a voluntarist, Gue-vara's voluntarism was based on a commitment to Marxist principles as he understood them and his own quixotic moral sense.[54] Fidel Castro's voluntarism stemmed from his huge political ambitions and caudillista political style, which led him to undertake economically irrational poli-cies involving gigantic projects such as the eight-lane (*ocho vias*) highway traversing much of the country, let alone the disastrous campaign for a ten-million-ton sugar crop in 1970. Yet, while Castro's voluntarism may have gotten him into trouble when he was in power—as in the case of the 1980 Mariel exodus—it may have helped him when he was leading the armed rebellion against Batista. It allowed him to maximize the objective and subjective political opportunities that the Cuba of the 1950s offered to successfully develop a revolutionary movement that mobilized the disaffection of large sectors of Cuban youth behind an intransigent and militant political strategy. At the same time, during the last stage of the struggle against Batista (1956–1958), Castro formulated a moderate social program that reassured the Cuban middle and upper classes.

Along with his cosmopolitan background, and his not being a native of Cuba, Guevara's distance from Argentinian nationalist politics may explain why his anti-imperialism was relatively less nationalist than that of the Cubans he joined in Mexico. It also explains why his internationalism was deeper than that of the Cuban leadership's and therefore not as wedded to the future of the island republic.

Chapter Two

Che Guevara's Revolutionary Politics: Ideas and Practices

Ernesto "Che" Guevara, the Independent Communist

In spite of hundreds of articles and books written about Ernesto "Che" Guevara, much remains to be clarified about his politics. That he became an iconic figure and symbol of rebellion has tended to obscure the substance of his thinking and political record. This is especially true in regards to the years he spent as a guerrilla fighter and, after the Cuban Revolution, as one of the top leaders in Cuba.

Liberal and radical progressive opinion, particularly in the United States, has often explained the evolution of the Cuban Revolution from a multiclass democratic revolt against dictatorship to a radical social revolution of the Communist type as merely a reaction to a "mistaken" US foreign policy. Thus, Maurice Zeitlin and Robert Scheer claimed in 1963 that "Cuba is an American tragedy. . . . If, in Cuba today, the chances for political democracy are slim, if Cuba accepts and imitates Soviet methods uncritically, and comes increasingly under Communist influence, if there may now be an end to civil liberties for some time to come, it is a result of our government's policies."[1] Aside from implicitly assuming that US foreign policy toward Cuba could have been substantially different and brushing aside the powerful structural obstacles that existed to an alternative policy, Zeitlin and Scheer treat the principal leaders of the Cuban Revolution—the Castro brothers and Che Guevara among others—as blank slates with no political ideas of their own. To be sure, these revolutionary leaders acted under serious external and internal constraints, but they were nevertheless autonomous agents pursuing their own independent ideological visions and not simply reacting to Washington's policies. These leaders made choices, including having deliberately chosen the Communist road for the Cuban Revolution. As Guevara himself told the French weekly *L'Express* on July 25, 1963, "Our commitment to the eastern bloc was half the fruit of constraint and half the result of choice."

Ernesto Guevara arrived in Guatemala at the end of 1953, and there he witnessed the overthrow of the democratically elected reform government of Jacobo Árbenz by forces organized and supported by the CIA. This experience deepened his political radicalism and converted him into a committed nonparty Communist, which implied an identification with the Soviet Union and the Communist model of the one-party state controlling almost all social, political, and economic aspects of the life of a country, leaving no place for opposition parties or independent voluntary associations. The hegemonic ideological and political role played by the Partido Guatemalteco del Trabajo (the name used at the time by the Guatemalan Communist Party) in the Guatemalan left during the dramatic events leading to the overthrow of Árbenz undoubtedly was an important factor explaining Guevara's adherence to Communist ideology at this time. When later that year he left for Mexico, he was no longer merely a radical. He was a Communist, though not affiliated with any party.

Although politically influenced by the Guatemalan Communists, Guevara angrily refused to join their party as a condition of being hired for a government job that was offered to him.[2] Neither did he join the Mexican Communist Party when he was an exile in that country. Even though he refused to join either party, Guevara had closely identified with Joseph Stalin from early on.[3] This identification with Stalin continued. When he visited the Soviet Union as a representative of the Cuban revolutionary government in November 1960, he insisted on depositing a floral tribute at Stalin's tomb against the advice of the Cuban government's ambassador to the Soviet Union.[4] The political significance of this gesture is underlined by the fact that it took place more than four years after Nikita Khrushchev's revelations of Stalin's crimes, when Stalin had become a reviled figure even within the Communist parties themselves.

However, during his political life, Guevara was critical of the Communist parties in general. He disliked the bureaucratic functioning and especially the conservatism of the pro-Moscow Communist parties in Latin America. That may help to explain why he remained an independent Communist. Guevara's politics were closer to the ultraleftist militancy of the Communist International's so-called Third Period of the late 1920s and early 1930s than to the political maneuvering of Popular Front politics with its cross-class alliances with the anti-right, anti-Fascist opposition, which the Comintern had established by the mid-1930s. It was this kinship with ultraleft Communism that also explains, as we shall see in greater detail in chapter 4, his criticism of Lenin for having introduced capitalist forms of competition in the Soviet Union with the New Economic Policy.[5] In contrast with Moscow's acceptance of the Cold War division of the world that left the Western hemisphere in the US sphere of influence, he was a strong advocate of spreading the revolution beyond Cuba to the rest of Latin America. This led many to compare Guevara with Leon Trotsky who, unlike Guevara, emphasized workers' democracy and the repudiation of the one-party state as key features of the socialist revolution.[6] It is true that during Guevara's tenure as minister of industry in Cuba, he got along with, and even protected, the Trotskyists who worked under him. But since these Trotskyists were supporters, even if critical ones, of the one-party state that had just been established in Cuba, Guevara saw them as revolutionaries who differed from him on important matters, but allies nevertheless. However, when shortly after the victory of the revolution (as we shall see in the next chapter) other revolutionaries, tried to organize within the July 26th movement against Raúl Castro's and Guevara's attempts, supported from outside the government by the old pro-Moscow Cuban Communist Party, to establish the one-party Soviet model in Cuba, Guevara and his political allies fought them aggressively.

Guevara was also critical of the dogmatic and narrow-minded "Marxism" transmitted by Soviet manuals, a sentiment that he extended to the cultural attitudes of "socialist realism" in the arts.[7] Although attracted to Stalinist-type Communism in terms of its socioeconomic and political structures, he rejected the Communist smugness that Moscow and the Communist Parties that followed its lead had propagated. This is one of the reasons that Guevara has been attractive to certain types of cultivated left intellectuals, particularly in the economically developed capitalist countries, who have also been more put off by the cultural philistinism of Moscow-style Communism than by the social and political features of the systems over which it ruled.

Another distinguishing feature of Guevara's independent Communism—that has also appealed to many—was the principled, consistent egalitarianism he displayed in his politics and personal life, whether as a guerrilla fighter in and out of Cuba or when in power. Guevara's leadership role in the Cuban government was relatively brief—from 1959 to 1965, during the initial years of the revolution. One might wonder what his reaction would have been if he had lived longer to see the emergence of privilege and inequality in Cuba. Although privilege and economic inequality are not the defining characteristics of the Communist system anymore than the unequal consumption and luxury of the bourgeoisie are the defining characteristics of capitalism, they have been the inevitable consequences of a system of class rule and a hierarchical social division of labor that has no institutional democratic controls from below and lacks a mechanism to renew the leadership that goes along with it. In that context, Guevara's idiosyncratic Communism and personality seems to have made him better suited to remain a Communist oppositionist than to become a long-term Communist ruler.[8]

Following a long political tradition, Guevara's egalitarianism left little room for individual differences or individual rights. In March 1960, he declared that "one has to constantly think on behalf of masses and not on behalf of individuals. . . . It's criminal to think of individuals because the needs of the individual becomes completely weakened in the face of the needs of the human conglomeration." In August 1964, when he had already become very critical of the Soviet Union, Che postulated that the individual "becomes happy to feel himself a cog in the wheel, a cog that has its own characteristics and is necessary though not indispensable, to the production process, a conscious cog, a cog that has its own motor, and that consciously tries to push itself harder and harder to carry to a happy conclusion one of the premises of the construction of socialism—creating a sufficient quantity of consumer goods for the entire population."[9] This is particularly jarring when one considers that around the world the student movement and radical workers were criticizing the notion that they were "cogs in the machine."[10]

Guevara's Voluntarism

One of the most noticeable elements of Guevara's idiosyncratic Communism, an element that had a deep impact on his political practice, was his voluntarism. In classical Marxism—and Guevara was well read in the literature of Marxism—historical change is the product of the interplay of objective and subjective factors that are in constant tension. It is expressed in Marx's well-known formulation in *The Eighteenth Brumaire of Louis Bonaparte*: "Men make their own history, but they do not make it just as they please; they do not make it under circumstances chosen by themselves, but under circumstances directly found, given and transmitted by the past."[11] "Ripe" economic and social conditions cannot by themselves bring about a revolution, but socialist revolutions don't happen under just any and all socioeconomic and political conditions. Under the best circumstances, those objective conditions can create a favorable situation that can be used to advantage by the active, conscious efforts of the revolutionary subject. The objective-subjective tension in Marx was abandoned by later tendencies claiming to be Marxist. German social democracy for example, elaborated a mechanical objectivism that minimized the subjective active element in history. Maoism, in contrast, presented an extreme version of voluntarism that completely ignored objective reality.

Moscow's official Communism and its parties propounded a deeply objectivist version of Marxism, similar to that of the SPD (Social Democratic Party) of Germany, that clashed with Guevara's voluntarism. His voluntarism became most explicit in two areas: political action and the economy. Regarding political action, Che adopted the view that guerrilla warfare was possible and desirable in every Latin American country regardless of existing sociopolitical and economic conditions. This view was closely related to his notion of internationalizing the revolution, which he summarized in the Cuban revolutionary slogan that the duty of the revolutionary was to make the revolution. Che's position may have been his response to the politics of many Latin American leftists, especially those associated with the pro-Moscow Communist parties in the almost twenty-five years preceding the Cuban Revolution. Political groups of the international left such as Guevaraists, Maoists, and most Trotskyists have tended to characterize these parties as reformist.[12] In doing so, they misapplied the traditional distinction between reform and revolution rooted in the disputes between social democracy and revolutionary Marxism, especially in the early part of the twentieth century, as if they were relevant to the historically different phenomenon of the Stalinized Communist parties of the Popular Front and later periods. The distinction between reformist and revolutionary was certainly not relevant to the Cuban Partido Socialista Popular (PSP), the traditional Cuban pro-Moscow party. On one hand, the PSP could be as involved in politicking as the traditional political parties and as conservative as the rest of the other pro-Moscow Communist parties in Latin America. So much so that in the mid-1940s it was one of the few Communist parties singled out by Jacques Duclos, the French Communist leader who hewed closest to the political line of the Soviet Union, for exemplifying the "right-wing" line of US Communist leader Earl Browder.[13] Yet, during the course of the Cuban Revolution, no important PSP figure showed any inclination or commitment to the preservation of the capitalist status quo. Nor did any of them break with Castro when the Cuban leader decided to move toward Communism, as was the case with the authentically reformist Cuban political groups and individuals.[14] It is true that on the whole PSP leaders tended to be more cautious than Fidel Castro but, sooner or later, they supported him in his anticapitalist measures. It is significant that the PSP was dissolved not because it joined the opposition to the Cuban regime, as was generally the case with the authentically reformist elements in Cuba, but because it merged with the July 26th movement and the Directorio Revolucionario to form the new Cuban Communist Party in the first half of the sixties.[15] So if the PSP, a traditional pro-Moscow party, behaved in this fashion, how could it have been regarded as reformist?

In reality, the traditional Communist parties were neither reformist nor revolutionary. They were Moscow-influenced bureaucratic machines guided, most of all, by the pursuit of power to be implemented by either "reformist" or "revolutionary" means pending on the circumstances. Only later, after the prolonged prosperity in the developed capitalist countries and major changes in the relations between the Soviet Union and the Western powers, did many of those Communist parties become truly reform parties, in the sense of working for reforms within a capitalist system that they now fully accepted, a development taken to its final conclusion by the collapse of the Soviet Union in the early 1990s, which led to the disappearance of many of these political organizations.

But even if we assume that the early twentieth-century traditional distinction between reform and revolution could apply to the pro-Moscow

Latin American Communist parties, Guevara misdiagnosed the problem. It was not, as he held, that these parties had failed to make the revolution, although that might have been the main problem at certain times and places, but rather that these parties, with their unprincipled maneuvering and politicking, did not behave as revolutionaries should in nonrevolutionary situations: advancing, instead of compromising, the revolutionary goal, primarily by preserving the independence of the working class and popular movements. Thus, through the early 1940s, the pro-Moscow Cuban Communists supported Batista's electoral coalition in exchange for control of the trade union movement, and in the process strengthened state control of union affairs.

The second area where Guevara's voluntarism became a salient element of his ideas and practice was in the economy, a dimension of material reality that, in contrast with the human consciousness that Guevara always emphasized, is relatively more resistant to change at least in the short term, and even more so in the context of scarcity. Thus, for example, while dislocation and disruption are essential political weapons in the promotion of revolutionary political and social change, other considerations come into play when it comes to the economy. It is true that the overturn of capitalist social relations in the economy requires agitation and disruption. But particularly after the initial revolutionary period has passed, balance, proportionality, and a conscious recognition of the limitations imposed by material reality—sources of raw materials, energy resources, and skill levels of workers, among other factors—become fundamental considerations to promote the revolutionary economic transformation, or at least to prevent economic regression. As Cuban minister of industry, Guevara promoted a policy of rapid industrialization for the period 1960–62.[16] As he proposed in 1960, "Cuba is a country of enormous wealth, it has everything it needs for industrialization. . . . In a few years we will have developed from an agricultural into an industrial state."[17] In mid-1961, he announced, on behalf of the revolutionary government, a highly unrealistic four-year economic plan with fantastical goals, such as a 15 percent annual growth rate, the tenfold multiplication of the production of fruits and other raw materials for the canning industry, an overall growth of food consumption of 12 percent annually, and the doubling of living standards in just four years.[18] He ignored crucial economic limitations, such as the shortage of raw materials, which often provoked stoppages at the workplaces for which they were destined. Cuba did not have coal and iron to produce steel or sufficient raw materials to make clothing and shoes. Some of these raw materials could be supplied by the Soviet bloc, but the rest had to be obtained from other countries. And Cuba lacked the foreign reserves needed to import from nations requiring hard-currency payments.[19] After much of the damage had been done, Guevara admitted, in March 1962, that he had designed "an absurd plan, disconnected from reality, with absurd goals and imaginary resources."[20]

The problem with grandiose, unrealistic economic plans is not only that they are nearly impossible to achieve but they may also seriously disrupt the economy and bring about regression instead of progress. Guevara's emphasis on the rapid industrialization of Cuba was one of the causes of the devastation of agriculture in the early 1960s. In the sugar sector, then the most important source of foreign reserves for the island, the cultivated area of sugar cane shrunk 25 percent below 1958 levels due to factors that included the government's hostility to sugar, the disorganization created by the administrative changes resulting from Guevara's industrializing policies, as well as a scarcity of professional sugarcane cutters, who had moved to easier jobs. The production of tobacco, coffee, beans, and tubers also declined, which meant that agricultural output was 23 percent below 1959 levels in 1963. During the same period, a lack of information and managerial control led to the loss of agricultural produce in the ground or after harvesting because of the lack of transportation. By 1963, Cuba was producing neither steel nor tractors, and its overall production of cement, electricity, and manufactured items such as cigars and beer had fallen below 1961 levels. Besides poor planning for the installation and integration of the newly built factories, the US economic blockade made it impossible to acquire spare parts and import new machinery, which along with the exodus of US and Cuban industrial managers and technicians, delivered a substantial blow to the efficient workings of the economy.[21]

The rapid shift from an economy oriented to the United States to one oriented to the Soviet block was also disruptive. As I discuss in greater detail in chapter 4, Guevara's insistence on establishing a system of highly centralized planning, which was based on ill-founded assumptions about Cuban society and economics, was not workable. Although Cuba was relatively advanced in communications (roads, telephones, and mass media), it lacked sufficient trained personnel (even without the exodus of engineers and technicians) to communicate reliable and timely economic information to the center, and the relatively small size and dispersion of its commercial and industrial plants added a great deal of complexity, difficulty, and inefficiency to the physical planning of production.

Guevara's Political Schematism and Indifference to Specific Contexts

Among the top Cuban revolutionary leaders who survived the struggle against Batista and the first year of the victorious revolution, Guevara was the most sophisticated in terms of Marxist theory and history. Fidel Castro was also a well-read man, but he was primarily a very shrewd political tactician and a man of action animated by a profound hunger for political leadership and power. Che was also unlike Raúl Castro, who, like Guevara, identified with Communism, but as a talented organizer rather than an intellectual or theoretician. In terms of political practice, Guevara lacked that hard-to-define but real trait called political instinct, and evinced a certain political tone-deafness, schematism, ignorance of, and indifference to specific political contexts, as with his assertion that practically the whole of Latin America was ready for guerrilla warfare. This is also evident in his inability to recognize specific political textures and historical conjunctures in Cuba during the period of armed struggle against the Batista dictatorship.

A telling example of Guevara's political tone-deafness was his proposal in 1958 to finance rebel operations by robbing banks. When that proposal was resisted by the urban leadership of the July 26th movement, Guevara took it as a sign of their social conservatism.[22] He wrote to "Sierra" [Enrique Oltuski], a leader of the movement in central Cuba, making the conjuncturally irrelevant argument that "those who make money by dealing with the money of others, by speculating with it, have no right to special consideration. The miserable sum they offer is what they make in a day of exploitation, while the suffering people are bled dry in both the Sierra and the plains."[23] What Guevara entirely overlooked was the specific meaning and consequences that bank robberies had in the Cuban context. He was apparently unaware that in the late 1940s and early 1950s, less than ten years earlier, Cuba had gone through a period when many of the revolutionaries of the 1930s had degenerated into nothing more than gangsters involved in violent activities, including the armed assault on and robbery of the Havana branch of the Royal Bank of Canada in 1948. Any involvement of the revolutionaries of the 1950s in such activities would have brought back memories of that dark period and would have been extremely damaging from a political point of view, particularly since Fidel Castro himself had been associated with those "action groups" during his student days at the University of Havana. The Batista press would have had a field day arguing that Fidel Castro had gone back to the practices of his youth and was returning the country to the bad old days of political gangsterism.[24]

It was with the same schematic approach and tactical blindness that Guevara approached the Sierra Maestra Manifesto that Fidel Castro signed with Felipe Pazos and Raúl Chibás, two important Cuban figures, on July 12, 1957.[25] Guevara expressed dissatisfaction with the agreement for being too moderate, although he allowed that, at that moment, it was necessary and progressive. This manifesto was a socially but not politically moderate document, but, most of all, it was a tactical stroke of genius by Fidel Castro. By endorsing the armed struggle of the July 26th movement against Batista, the manifesto legitimated the revolutionary movement among the broad, progressive anti-Batista public at a time when it was only beginning to consolidate itself in the Sierra Maestra. Moreover, the publication of the document in *Bohemia*, the Cuban magazine with the largest circulation on the island, at a moment when censorship had been suspended, electrified hundreds of thousands of people and helped Fidel Castro and his movement attain an unrivaled hegemony in the opposition camp. Contrary to Guevara's assertions that Raúl Chibás (brother of Eduardo Chibás, the deceased founder of the Partido Ortodoxo) and Felipe Pazos were "distinguished representatives of the Cuban oligarchy" and "two cavemen," suggesting hard right-wing politics, the two men were actually moderate liberal reformers with a reputation for honesty, not a minor issue in the Cuban political culture of the period. In fact, had they been representatives of the Cuban oligarchy, they would not have been able to fulfill the political role Fidel Castro successfully assigned to them at that moment.

Guevara's critique of the 1957 pact might have also been somewhat disingenuous since he wrote it only after the victory of the revolution, and very likely after the enactment of the radical Agrarian Reform law of May 1959, thus making the land reform proposals of the 1957 pact appear more conservative than they had been at the time. Along the same lines, Guevara also ignored the critical fact that no significant political force had proposed anything more radical than that pact before Batista's overthrow on December 31, 1958. One example is the critical issue of compensation to the former owners of the land. In 1958, the Workers' Bureau of the reputedly more left-wing Second Front led by Raúl Castro in Oriente Province declared itself in favor of agrarian reform but abstained from specifying the concrete policy terms of that reform and entirely avoided the issue of compensation for the land seized by the state.[26] Similarly, the PSP (Partido Socialista Popular, the pro-Moscow Communists) published a program in December 1958 entitled "The Right Solution for Cuba" ("La Solución que Conviene a Cuba") that proposed, among other things, an unspecified program of agrarian reform that did not even allude to the requirement in the 1940 Constitution for "previous payment" to the dispossessed owners, a proviso that the Communists had strongly criticized during the convention that drafted the Constitution eighteen years earlier.[27] The main difference between the document signed by Fidel Castro, Pazos, and Chibás and the program of what retrospectively could be considered to have been the leftwing of the movement was that the pact explicitly supported the constitutional provision for compensation while the more radical elements avoided any reference to the issue. None of this was surprising, however, since in the period of 1956–58, Fidel Castro had set aside his 1953 radical agenda of "History Will Absolve Me," which was in fact little known at that time, for the sake of building broad support for his politically militant but socially moderate program. Besides, since the revolutionaries of all stripes were at the time advocating the restoration of the generally progressive 1940 Constitution, they were unlikely to attack one of its important provisions.[28] But it seems that Guevara was indifferent to the concrete historical record and political meaning of this period.

Guevara and Guerrilla Warfare in Cuba

Nowhere does the interplay of political ideas and practice that characterized Guevara's thought come out so clearly as in his leading role in guerrilla warfare in Cuba. As he described it in *Reminiscences of the Cuban Revolutionary War*, he met Fidel Castro for the first time in Mexico City on a cold night in 1955.[29] They struck up a conversation that evolved into a discussion of international politics. By dawn, Guevara had become a member of the group that would land with Fidel Castro in Cuba in late 1956. The classes on military tactics that he and other future fighters took in Mexico from General Alberto Bayo (one of the hundreds of Cuban-born veterans of the loyalist Republican Army in the Spanish Civil War) convinced Guevara that victory was in fact possible, since, as he frankly admitted, initially victory "had seemed doubtful when I first enrolled with the rebel commander, to whom I was attached from the beginning by a leaning toward romantic adventure and the notion that it would be well worth dying on a foreign beach for such pure ideals."[30]

When the boat *Granma* departed from the Mexican port of Tuxpan toward eastern Cuba shortly after midnight on November 25, 1956, Ernesto Guevara was one of a group of eighty-two men that quite deliberately only included four non-Cubans.[31] He was the group's doctor and a second-rank leader, rather than one of its principal commanders. The immediate purpose of the expedition was to provide support and extend the uprising that according to plan took place on November 30 in Santiago de Cuba, the principal city in eastern Cuba and one of the largest on the island, an uprising that was defeated by Batista's army. The *Granma* landed considerably west of Santiago, in another part of Oriente province, on December 2, and was two days late. Its contingent was decimated shortly afterward by government forces. The twenty-two survivors—including those who were able to regroup fairly quickly and the few others who were eventually able to rejoin the main group—took refuge in the nearby Sierra Maestra mountain range. Fleeing to the Sierra Maestra was not the preferred option of the expeditionaries, but was a previously agreed upon fallback plan if the landing failed.[32] While physically isolated in the Sierra Maestra, they were not politically isolated: their connection to the substantial national urban network of the July 26th movement permitted them to survive and grow. Frank País, the leader of the failed uprising of November 30 in Santiago de Cuba, organized a group of thirty armed and twenty unarmed people—a considerably larger group than the *Granma* survivors—who arrived on March 16, 1957, to reinforce the small rebel group.[33]

During the comparatively short armed campaign (1957–58) to overthrow Batista's dictatorship, Guevara attained the highest possible rank of major and became one of the principal leaders of the rebel army due to his military courage, ability, and leadership, a calling and activity that he clearly preferred to serving as doctor. Unlike Fidel and Raúl Castro, Che was open about his political ideas and worldview. In response to the "third camp" sentiments opposing the policies of both Washington and Moscow expressed by "Daniel" [Major René Ramos Latour], who was later killed in the Sierra and whose politics Paco Ignacio Taibo II described as "radical workerist nationalist," Guevara wrote on December 14, 1957 (in a letter that Che himself would later describe as "rather idiotic" without explaining why) that "because of my ideological background I belong to those who believe that the solution to the world's problems are behind the so-called Iron Curtain and I see this [July 26th] movement as one of the many provoked by the eagerness of the bourgeoisie to get rid of the economic chains of imperialism. I always considered Fidel [Castro] an authentic leader of the left-wing of the bourgeoisie, although his figure is enhanced by personal qualities of an extraordinary brilliance that place him well above his class."[34]

It was in the Sierra Maestra that Che began a political relationship with the PSP, which around that time had shifted its political orientation toward reaching a rapprochement with the guerrilla movement. The relationship became so close that when Che founded his first school for the political instruction of cadres in the Sierra Maestra, he asked the PSP to send him its first political instructor. The PSP sent Pablo Ribalta, a young but experienced Black Cuban party militant who would, years later, become Cuba's ambassador to Tanzania and thus Che's principal conduit to Havana when Guevara was engaged in guerrilla warfare in the Congo.[35] Guevara's close collaboration with the PSP lasted for almost four years, including the critical years of the development and consolidation of Cuba's Communist system. Then in the early to mid-1960s, Che broke with Moscow and the traditional Latin American Communist parties, at the time that the PSP was in the process of joining with the July 26th movement and the Directorio Revolucionario to form the new Cuban Communist Party in 1965.[36]

The "Sierra" and the "Llano"

During the two-year guerrilla struggle, a number of tensions and conflicts developed between the rebel leadership in the Sierra Maestra and the urban underground—the so-called confrontation between the *sierra* (mountain range) and the *llano* (plains or urban areas)—generally seen as having been based on tactical and strategic differences over the struggle against Batista. In this conflict, Guevara emerged as the principal proponent of the sierra position. Guevara interpreted the conflict as one based on social class differences, a view that later on he elaborated in the prologue to the book *El Partido Marxista Leninista*, published in 1963, arguing that "the Rebel Army was already ideologically proletarian and thought of as a dispossessed class; the urban leadership remained petty bourgeois, with future traitors among its leaders and greatly influenced by the milieu in which it developed."[37] It was this view that informed much of his discussion with the llano rebels.

A close look at the differences between the sierra and the llano seriously calls into question Guevara's interpretation. In the first place, the most enduring element behind the tensions between the sierra and the llano were not strategic or tactical differences as such, but a perennial struggle over the distribution of scarce resources between the sierra rebels and the urban underground, particularly concerning weapons, munitions, and other indispensable elements of warfare. Among the many tasks assigned by the sierra leadership to the urban underground was deterring the phony presidential elections that the government was preparing and setting the stage for the general strike. "Daniel" complained to Fidel Castro about this in February 1958, indicating that "we require them [the chiefs of action in the cities] to keep up sabotage, armed action, and agitation; we tell them that it is they who will have to provoke and sustain the strike and they know they cannot do this with their hands or with rocks. There have been many victims already."[38] "Daniel" had agreed to try to lend a hand with uniforms, backpacks, and bullets, but he wanted to keep some of the mortars in the cities to be used against military barracks and electrical plants,[39] thus confronting the sierra leadership's tendency to monopolize scarce military resources.

In addition, Fidel Castro succeeded in creating a cohesive group around himself in the Sierra Maestra, which, contrary to Guevara's subsequent claim about the proletarian ideology prevailing in the rebel army, was based not on any particular ideology of social revolution but on an intransigent line of militant political opposition to the Batista dictatorship and on maximizing Castro's personal control over the whole movement in the sierra and, as much as possible, in the llano. As Carlos Franqui noted in the "Theses" he presented to the last meeting of the national leadership of the July 26th movement held in the Sierra Maestra in October 1958: "I have observed that many of our meetings are in fact a species of consultation. Or a conversation, almost always the prodigious conversation of Fidel, in which a decision is taken for granted, while an agreement discussed in depth among ourselves is almost never taken. This is a situation for which all of us are responsible either by commission or by omission."[40] Thus, while there was a strong dominant leader in the sierra, there was no parallel united leadership in the llano, a result of the fact that the llano forces, distributed throughout the whole country, were far more socially and politically diverse than those in the sierra, rendering Guevara's attempt to label the urban leadership as a whole petty bourgeois untenable. The sierra was not a social category as Guevara argued, but a political category based on control: the sierra was equivalent to Fidel Castro and Fidel Castro was equivalent to the sierra.

It is worth noting that as a general rule the peasants recruited to the rebel army in the Sierra Maestra did not play the leading political policy-making roles in the Rebel Army, or in the July 26th movement, either before or after the revolution. It is true that a few of these peasants, such as Guillermo García Frías, rose to the highest ranks in the rebel army and the government bureaucracy. That was also the case of Juan Vitalio Acuña Nuñez (Vilo Acuña), another peasant who rose to become a member of the Central Committee of the Cuban Communist Party and died in Bolivia as a member of the group that accompanied Che to that country. However, the case of Crescencio Pérez, the single most prominent of the peasant leaders who played an indispensable role in protecting the survivors from the *Granma* and providing them with contacts in the region, is particularly instructive. Although he rose to the highest rank of major in the rebel army, he played virtually no role in the revolutionary government after the victory of January 1, 1959. However, many of the rebels who came from cities and towns in Oriente province, and were not peasants, did play leading roles, as was the case with Celia Sánchez Manduley, Fidel Castro's principal aide and confidant. She was a doctor's daughter active in the July 26th movement in Manzanillo, one of Oriente's principal cities.[41] While there was a tension and conflict between the sierra and the llano, this could not be validly interpreted in social, let alone class, terms, but must be understood in political terms.

The Question of the Communists

Another important source of tension between Guevara and the llano leadership of the July 26th movement was the question of how to relate to the PSP (Partido Socialista Popular), the Moscow-oriented Cuban Communist Party. This was a party that had lost a lot of ground since the Cold War began in the mid- to late 1940s. Although the Cuban Communists had been the predominant political force in the Cuban labor movement in the 1930s and early 1940s, by the time the rebels began to fight the Batista dictatorship in the Sierra Maestra, they had become much weaker. A 1956 PSP internal report revealed that only 15 percent of the country's two thousand local unions were led by Communists or by union leaders who supported collaboration with the PSP.[42] The Communists' policies and tactics varied greatly during the Batista regime. Until 1957, the PSP's policies had been close to those of the moderate opposition. However, by late 1957, they decided to support the armed struggle, and by the middle of the following year the PSP had reached a quiet and unpublicized agreement with Fidel Castro to collaborate with the July 26th movement.

Most of the July 26th movement resisted collaboration with the Communists. While some of this resistance can undoubtedly be explained by the social conservatism and Cold War ideology that prevailed among many of the politically militant opponents of Batista, it would be a serious mistake to see this as the main explanation for this phenomenon. In the first place, there was a generalized rivalry among the various rebel groups that, besides the PSP and the July 26th movement, included the Directorio Revolucionario (DR), the revolutionary organization founded by student activists at the University of Havana, which at various times had serious frictions with the July 26th movement. Moreover, the July 26th movement militants had well-founded political reasons for distrusting the PSP. Ever since it was founded in 1925, the Cuban Communist Party accumulated an ample record of sectarian and unprincipled politicking that led to a serious and enduring split in the Cuban left. As I indicated earlier, the PSP supported Batista in his earlier period of government from 1938 to 1944 in exchange for being allowed to control the unions. It did not support the attack on the Moncada Barracks that Fidel Castro organized on July 26, 1953, and characterized it as a putsch. Besides, the activists in the July 26th movement were Cuban nationalists who, like the activists of other revolutionary organizations such as the DR, disliked the PSP's blind adherence to Moscow's political line, particularly in the international arena. Moreover, as members of a politically loose and amorphous movement, the July 26th urban activists were nervous about collaborating with a hard and disciplined group that was not internally democratic and often hid its politics when operating inside larger political organizations.[43] It is worth noting that while Guevara perceived the differences between the sierra and the llano in class terms, with the sierra being proletarian and the llano petty bourgeois, one of the principal criticisms he made of the July 26th urban activists of the sierra was that they had refused to collaborate with the PSP, itself an overwhelmingly urban political organization with a significant working-class membership.[44]

The Failure of the April 1958 Strike and the Strategic Turn Toward the Sierra

The ongoing rift between the sierra and the llano came to a head over the failure of the general strike called by the July 26th movement on April 9, 1958. This defeat led to the complete domination of the sierra leadership over the July 26th movement, and to a major strategic change regarding the role of the general strike in the struggle against the Batista dictatorship. In this process, Guevara once more became the most prominent articulator of the sierra perspective and politics versus the llano.

Other strike attempts had preceded the April 1958 strike, including those of the bank workers' union and of the union of electricity workers, who had engaged in bitter walkouts that had strong overtones of hostility to the dictatorship. The same was true of the 1955 sugar strike in the three eastern provinces of Cuba. An unanticipated work stoppage broke out shortly after July 26th movement leader Frank País was killed by the Batista police in Santiago de Cuba on July 30, 1957. The results were impressive, as many towns and cities throughout the island, though not the capital, were almost completely paralyzed, at least for a short period of time.

It was the promising results of the August 1957 strike that led the July 26th movement leadership to organize the next strike. While the exact timing and other organizational details of the strike were left to the llano leadership, the conception of the strike itself was a joint product of the sierra and llano leaders. Although a strike call would be issued, asking workers to walk out of their jobs, the walkout would primarily rely on an armed urban insurrection that would create massive disruption aimed at stopping public transport to prevent workers from going to work. That is why the disruption was planned from noon to 2 p.m., when workers went home for lunch. But as Ramón Bonachea and Marta San Martín vividly describe, tactical errors seemed to have doomed the strike from the very beginning:

> During these two hours, the Youth brigade would attack the [Havana] armory, arms would be distributed, and street fighting would create panic and confusion. Urban transportation would be stopped, and people would be unable to return to their jobs even if they wished to do so. At 11 a.m. the strike order rang loud and clear through clandestine radios and from headquarters to the Youth Brigade. Dismay, outcry and frustration permeated the ranks of the M-26-7 [July 26th movement] underground when they were forced to move their entire schedule one hour ahead.[45]

A report submitted to Fidel Castro in May 1958 by a group of July 26th movement militia captains and workers' coordinators who participated in the strike indicated that there had been no other way to get workers to stay out of work and to prevent them from returning after lunch. According to the report, "The mass of the workers would have understood no other language . . . since they evidently seem to have a sort of mental attitude that demands 'revolutionary action' as an 'excuse' to vacate their jobs, as well as the [backing] of a strong organization as further guarantees."[46]

Underlying this attitude of the July 26th movement cadres was the considerable gap that had developed between the armed struggle and the workers' struggle against the dictatorship. Although approximately half of the Cuban working class was organized in unions, these institutions were hobbled by a corrupt labor bureaucracy that collaborated with the Batista dictatorship. And as the May report implied, there were no labor sections of the revolutionary opposition strong enough to protect the workers from the employers' or the government's response. It is true that the small but politically experienced Communist working-class cadre was not included in the preparation of the strike and did not as a result support it. But while the Communists would have surely made some difference, it is doubtful that it would have been enough to turn defeat into victory, since they only controlled at most 15 percent of the unions.

In spite of all these problems, the strike spread very widely. As described by Jules Dubois, the strike was total in most interior cities. But there was no general strike in Havana. Some factories closed there, and some bus lines stopped or offered only limited service. Batista's spy services and the countermeasures the dictator had taken, together with the failure of the rebels to take over and hold any radio stations, sealed the fate of the April strike.[47] There was a crucial difference between Havana and a city like Santiago de Cuba. Santiago had a strong sense of community, a kind of social cohesion that made strong workplace organization less essential than it was in the larger city of Havana. In metropolitan Havana, given the strike organizers' failure to secure any radio stations, only the presence of well-organized factory cells could have provided the organizational framework for the otherwise atomized workers. Thus, the issue was not, as some have implied, that workers were not sympathetic to the rebels by 1958. The issue was that, although the workers individually sympathized with the rebels, they had no organizational means to articulate opposition to the dictatorship in organized, class terms.

The Strategic Turn after the Defeat of the April 1958 Strike

On May 3, 1958, less than a month after the defeat of the April strike, eleven members of the July 26th movement leadership, including Che Guevara, met with Fidel Castro for two days at a tense and conflict-ridden meeting at Altos de Mompié in the Sierra Maestra to discuss the failure of the strike and how to proceed with the struggle.[48] At that meeting, it was Che Guevara who best articulated the sierra's political critique of the llano. He reiterated his earlier criticism, similar to the PSP's, that the strike had been badly prepared for a number of reasons, one of them being the exclusion of the PSP for its planning and execution. He attacked llano leader David Salvador, the workers' leader of the July 26th movement, for having acted in a sectarian fashion by excluding the PSP and subordinating other organizations to the decisions of the July 26th movement. Guevara also blamed llano leader Faustino Pérez for having ordered the July 26th movement militia to seize the capital in spite of the ample superiority enjoyed by Batista's police, and recriminated another July 26th movement leader, "Daniel," for having attempted to create an army parallel to that of the sierra "without the training or the combat morale, and without having gone through the rigorous process of selection in the war," in other words, for not being like the rebel army.[49] It is worth noting that all the leaders criticized by Guevara were hostile to the politics of the PSP (of which Salvador had been a former member). Guevara's arguments, shared by Fidel and Raúl Castro, won the day.

As a result, Fidel Castro assumed total control of the July 26th movement after the Mompié meeting. He became the head of a unified command as general secretary of the movement and commander in chief of the rebel army. The struggle of the urban underground was downgraded and, instead of the strike, guerrilla warfare became the movement's central military strategy.[50] For Che Guevara, the long meeting at Mompié confirmed the predominance of the sierra as a consequence of its "correct" point of view and its accurate interpretation of events, as well as the llano leadership's failure in April. He noted that it had been the sierra adherents, especially he and Raúl Castro, who had objected to the strike and predicted its failure. From then on, guerrilla warfare would become the only strategy, and the general strike would only come into play as the popular culmination of the military campaign.[51] That was exactly the strategy that led to the successful overthrow of the Batista dictatorship eight months later, although at a high cost in terms of the lack of autonomy of the July 26th movement and its complete subordination to Fidel Castro. After Batista's summer offensive was defeated in the Sierra Maestra, rebel columns led by Che Guevara and Camilo Cienfuegos rapidly moved west into central Cuba and by the end of December had defeated a demoralized army that by and large had little interest in fighting. After Batista and his immediate entourage fled the country on New Year's Day in 1959, there was a planned general strike to paralyze the country and make it very difficult for a military coup to take place. The general strike turned out to be more of a national celebration than an instrument of struggle.

The Evolution of Guevara's View of Guerrilla Warfare

In 1960, a little more than a year after the revolutionary victory and during the time he held leading positions in the revolutionary government, Che Guevara published a book titled *Guerrilla Warfare*. Contrary to what one might expect in the light of subsequent controversies, there is relatively little theoretical discussion in this work. It is a relatively modest attempt to articulate his thoughts about guerrilla warfare based on the Cuban experience. Most of it is actually a guerrilla warfare manual discussing the requisite conditions to conduct this kind of armed struggle and presenting many suggestions on issues ranging from major tactical questions about when to form new columns and avoid overextending the guerrilla army across too much territory to making sure that the guerrilla soldiers wear sensible shoes and hammocks have nylon covers that can be used to shield them from the rain.[52]

Che does, however, elaborate on some practical issues with political and moral implications. For instance, in discussing the different kinds of rebel military operations, he differentiates between sabotage, which he favors, and terrorism, which he regards as a "measure that it is generally ineffective and indiscriminate in its results, since it often makes victims of innocent people and destroys a large number of lives that could be valuable to the revolution."[53] The guerrilla army has to be careful in its relations and interactions with the population of the area within which it operates, lest its members be perceived as parasites or exploiters. Thus, any merchandise acquired or appropriated by the rebels should be paid for with cash, and if the rebels are short on cash, they should pay with bonds, which are to be redeemed at the first opportunity.[54] Nevertheless, some of his elaborations are problematic. Although surely one should expect guerrilla soldiers to have an exemplary moral conduct and "rigid" self-control to prevent a single excess or slip, his imperative that "the guerrilla soldier should be an ascetic" seems to be too much of a reflection of Guevara's personal moral and political values and has implications that go beyond the specific conditions of guerrilla warfare.[55]

This is also true of his discussion of the role of women in guerrilla warfare. Guevara acknowledges that women are capable of fighting alongside the men and recognizes the "extraordinary importance" of women in the development of the revolutionary process while criticizing the discrimination against them rooted in the colonial mentality "in all our countries."[56] Nevertheless, he ends up emphasizing their role in guerrilla warfare as messengers or couriers, as well as cooks to "greatly improve the diet," noting that in general "it is easier to keep [them] in these domestic tasks."[57] Guevara attempts to elevate the status of the guerrilla women's domestic labor, noting that one of the problems in guerrilla bands is that all works of a civilian character are scorned because combat roles are much preferred by the men.[58] The problem with Guevara's approach, however, is that it accepts patriarchal patterns and men's and women's historic gender roles, failing to challenge the men's disdain for domestic labor, which is of course unrelated to any physical differences between men and women. Thus, the gendered division of labor will largely prevail in the guerrilla band unless consciously challenged.

Nowhere in this extensive exposition on guerrilla warfare does Guevara discuss or even allude to the principle of electing the guerrilla leadership, at least to positions that are primarily political in nature. Elsewhere he affirmed as an axiom that needed no evidence or further argumentation that "revolutionary democracy had never been applied in the running of armies anywhere in the world, and that any attempt to implement it had ended in disaster."[59] Although the actual conduct of battles and other military operations are not compatible with democratic deliberation and voting, this hardly exhausts key activities of a guerrilla army, like the daily government and administration of non-combatant populations in the territories it controls.

Notwithstanding its modest theoretical reach, *Guerrilla Warfare* articulates what has become Guevara's most significant contribution to revolutionary thought and practice: his theory of guerrilla warfare and the conditions to conduct this kind of struggle. According to Guevara, the Cuban Revolution contributed three fundamental lessons to revolutionary movements in the American continent: 1) Popular forces can win a war against the army; 2) It is not necessary to wait until all conditions for making revolution exist; the insurrection can create them; and 3) in the underdeveloped Americas, the countryside is the basic area for armed fighting.[60]

Based fairly closely on the Cuban experience of the struggle against Batista, Guevara warned that it is not possible in the first phases of the war, probably because of the unfavorable balance of forces, to attempt any changes in the social order and that, during this stage, the rich should be bothered as little as possible.[61] Most important of all, he underlines that if a government has come to power through some form of popular vote and has some appearance of constitutional legality, the guerrilla struggle cannot be promoted, "since the possibilities of peaceful struggle have not yet been exhausted."[62] Two years after the publication of *Guerrilla Warfare*, when Guevara was still in power, he gave a speech to the Department of State Security, identifying an additional set of conditions that revolutionaries in other countries should consider before following the Cuban model of guerrilla warfare: the extent of imperialist penetration, the geographical distance from the Yankee metropolis, and the degree of influence of Cuban revolutionary ideas in that country.[63]

Of course there were other factors besides those mentioned by Guevara that made the Cuban case unique. While economically important, the Cuban capitalist class was politically weak, which means that there was no politically savvy Cuban oligarchy in any meaningful sense of the term to act as social and political protectors of the capitalist system.[64] Unlike what happened in other Latin American movements against dictatorship in the 1940s and 1950s, the collapse of the traditional political parties and the major defeats suffered by other revolutionary groups greatly facilitated the rise and hegemony of the July 26th movement. The mercenary character of the army, which was noted by Guevara elsewhere, was also very important.[65] It explains the failure of the attempt by the academy-trained professional army officers—the so-called *puros* (the pure)—to overthrow the Batista regime in 1956 and, more important, the general apathy and unwillingness of the soldiers to fight the rebels. Therefore, there is a sense in which the Cuban rebels did not really win *against* the army, so Guevara's conclusion that it is possible for popular forces to win a war against established armies is not an entirely valid generalization from the Cuban case and ignores the history of many revolutions that suggest that it is not so much the military defeat of government armies as their internal divisions and political disaffection among their ranks that leads them to defeat.

Whether or not the Cuban model and its peculiarities could have been replicated did not preclude the advent of social revolution elsewhere in Latin America. In 1979, for example, the Nicaraguan Revolution overthrew the Anastasio Somoza dictatorship, relying primarily on urban uprisings to succeed, while the attempt to establish "focos" on the Cuban model completely failed. Although there were still some similarities between the Nicaraguan and Cuban Revolutions, such as the multiclass character of both revolutions, at least in the insurrectionary stage, the Sandinista rebels did not follow Guevara's prescriptions in their fundamental outline.[66]

As the revolutionary process continued in the Cuba of the 1960s, Guevara's approach to guerrilla warfare hardened and in the process left behind many of the conditional statements he had put forward earlier in the decade. Thus, by 1963, he was beginning to dismiss his earlier notion that the existence of elected constitutional governments was an obstacle to the development of guerrilla warfare, although he still allowed that there might be countries where different conditions might require alternative courses of action.[67] However, by April 1967, in the "Message to the Tricontinental" that Che sent from Bolivia, he proclaimed that "almost every country in this continent is ripe for a type of struggle [meaning guerrilla struggle] that, in order to achieve victory, cannot be content with anything less than establishing a government of a socialist nature."[68] Why this change in Guevara's approach? When Guevara wrote *Guerrilla Warfare*, Fidel Castro had not yet declared the "socialist" character of the revolution, nor had the US- sponsored invasion of Cuba in April 1961 and missile crisis of October 1962 yet taken place. The diplomatic relations of all Latin American countries with Cuba, except for Mexico, had not yet evaporated under Washington's pressure. The serious economic crisis that began to affect the island in the early 1960s, partly as a result of the US economic blockade, had not yet happened either. But as all these events began to take place, they created among the Cuban leaders a certain degree of anxiety and urgency, and even a sense of political despair that made them, Guevara included, want to fight anywhere, regardless of the circumstances.

Guerrilla Warfare without a Social Base: The Congo

Consistent with his politics of internationalizing the revolution, Che Guevara not only partook in his government's effort to prepare and actively aid guerrilla warfare in countries such as Venezuela, but he also volunteered in April 1965 to personally lead a secret mission to support a rebellion in the Congo [then called Zaire]. Unlike the much smaller future operation in Bolivia in 1967, this represented a substantial undertaking for the Cuban government, undoubtedly facilitated by the Soviet Union's favorable view toward Cuban intervention in Africa, in contrast with its general opposition to Cuban operations in Latin America, which clearly violated the understanding between the two superpowers about respecting each other's spheres of influence.

A "column" of 120 men was very gradually sent to Tanzania, to be shipped across Lake Tanganyika into the Congo proper, and a second "column" of two hundred men was sent to the other side of the continent, near Brazzaville, the capital of Congo-Brazzaville, across the Congo River from

Leopoldville-Kinshasa, the capital of the Congo-Zaire.[69] Guevara and the Cubans who arrived in Tanzania crossed Lake Tanganyika to support a rebellion in the eastern Congo against the right-wing government of Prime Minister Moise Tshombe and President Joseph Kasavubu, propped up by the Western imperial powers. This rebellion had gathered momentum in mid-1964 and at its peak controlled one-third of Zaire. But Washington intervened, and by April 1965, when Guevara and his group of Cubans arrived, the mercenary leader Mike Hoare and his troops had succeeded in reducing the rebel territory to the region of Fizi-Baraka, which stretched for about a hundred miles along the western shores of Lake Tanganyika and about fifty miles inland, with only a few other isolated pockets that the mercenaries would eliminate in the next few weeks.[70]

After Guevara and the Cubans left the Congo later that year, Che wrote an impressive and remarkable account of the expedition for the exclusive use of the Cuban leaders that was only made public more than thirty years later.[71] Without pulling any punches, Guevara characterized the Congo expedition, in the very first sentence of his account, as "the history of a failure."[72] Part of the failure was due to the role played by Cuba's ally, the People's Liberation Army (PLA), a parasitic army that did not work, train, or fight and yet lived off the population and was led by leaders that, with a few honorable exceptions, were also parasitic and did no fighting.[73] Moreover, although he did not put it in those words, Guevara acknowledged that the PLA had no social base and its popular support was at best uncertain. Guevara also discovered a PLA that lacked organization and had little discipline and politico-ideological development.[74] Not surprisingly, he noted that many Cuban soldiers, including members of the Cuban Communist Party, became demoralized by the experience, a state he characterized as "Congolization," by which he meant the absorption among the members of the Cuban contingent of a "series of habits and attitudes to the revolution that characterized the Congolese soldier at those moments of the struggle."[75] In response, many of the Cuban combatants only wanted to leave Africa and return to Cuba.[76]

A superficial reader could perceive Guevara's description of the Congolese soldiers as racist. He despairs of the Congolese soldiers' belief that the *dawa* medicine they took made them invulnerable to gunfire. Many treated the dawa as an article of faith, and even the most politically advanced rebels claimed that it was a natural, material force whose power they, as dialectical materialists, had to recognize.[77] In addition, Congolese soldiers refused, for superstitious reasons, to stay in trenches that they had dug themselves and thus abandoned any solid defense against attack. However, in contrast with the casual racism of his pre-Communist early adulthood—when he wrote about "the African race who have maintained their racial purity thanks to their lack of an affinity with bathing" and how in contrast with the European who "has a tradition of work and saving" the Black "is indolent and a dreamer; spending his meager wage on frivolity and drink"[78]—the Guevara of the mid-1960s was a careful defender of the Africans and always tried to explain their weaknesses.[79] He attributed the Congolese fighters' counterproductive beliefs and practices not to any racial essence but to the economic and social backwardness and low level of development of the country, at least in comparison to Cuba at the time of the revolution against Batista.[80] This does not mean that there was no truth behind the words attributed to Egyptian president Nasser, when Guevara told him that he was going to lead a group of Black Cubans to fight in the Congo, warning Guevara not to become "another Tarzan, a white man among Black men, leading them and protecting them. . . . It can't be done."[81] In a sense, Guevara acknowledged this when he wrote about the Cubans' sharp treatment of the African commanders, the Africans' ignorance and superstition, their inferiority complex, the way the Cubans offended their sentiments, and even the pain they must have felt when a white man scolded them, as in the colonial days.[82] Guevara admits too that there was favoritism and a certain degree of discrimination by the Cubans against the Congolese. He related having heard a Black Cuban soldier say, "Send me two of those Blacks over there," meaning two Congolese, and concluded that the Cubans failed to establish "entirely fraternal relations, and we feel a little bit like superior people who have to give advice."[83]

The "People's War" in the Eastern Congo—No Social Basis for a Political Program

In addition to describing the guerrilla's "people's war" in the Congo as exploiting rather than being connected with the people, Che Guevara makes an astonishing observation in his evaluation:

> In all wars of liberation of this type, a basic element is the hunger for land. . . . In the Congo, however, this was not the case—at least not

in our region, and probably not in most of the country. . . . On the eastern front [where Guevara's Cuban contingent operated], there is no significant land hunger or even individual enclosures; mere convention ensures that the crop belong [sic] to those who grow it. Nor, in practice, is property defended against intruders; only where there are some gardens is there a little protection against goats and other animals that might cause damage. The concept of land ownership hardly exists in any of the areas we visited, and the huge expanses of the Congo Basin permit anyone who wishes to acquire land simply to go and work there. As far as I can gather, in the area around Bukavu to the north, feudalism is much more developed and there are real feudal lords and serfs, but in the mountainous region where we lived the peasants are completely independent.[84]

He notes that imperialism did not really play much of a role in the region. Outside powers were mostly interested in the strategic mineral resources of Katanga, which had an industrial proletariat, in the diamonds found in Katanga and Kasai, and in the tin deposits close to the area where he operated, but not inside it. Guevara explicitly admitted having always been bothered by the question of what the liberation army had to offer these peasants. It could have possibly protected the population from the gross mistreatment—rapes of women, killings of men, women, and children, and forced requisition of food and other services—that they suffered at the hands of the government troops. But this was very limited. Guevara knew that the liberation army did not offer much protection or education, only the modicum of health care that the Cuban troops were able to provide.[85]

In other words, Che admitted that the Congolese revolution supposedly being carried out by the PLA did not and could not have a social program, which from a Marxist point of view made the Cuban intervention superfluous and irrelevant, although it could have perhaps been justified by the realpolitik and Cold War politics of Africa's heads of state, which had little or nothing to do with working-class internationalism, socialism, or Marxism.[86] Yet, his honest account of an objective situation, of a war without resonance in the population and with no program to propose, did not lead him to conclude that the Cuban government had made a mistake in getting involved in the eastern Congo or that at least it would be necessary in the future to pay much closer attention to the socioeconomic and political conditions in an area before considering

Cuba's involvement in guerrilla warfare. Having starkly presented the problem of the absence of a social base for guerrilla warfare, Guevara changed the subject in order to avoid drawing any political conclusions that might have put into question the rationale for Cuban intervention. Instead, he proposed that since the Congolese had no faith in their leaders, it was necessary to develop a party to lead the revolution at the national level, "a task which itself requires a capable, heroic and farsighted team of leaders."[87] Guevara added that the link with the workers would be achieved at a later stage. He also affirmed the "so-called worker-peasant alliance" by which he meant the "alliance of the highly backward peasantry with the ideology of the proletariat," substituting the actual working class for its supposed ideology upheld by the Communist Party.[88] Later, he argued, the industrial workers who are privileged in their exploitation would close ranks with the guerrilla movement as a result of the catalyzing effect of armed activity.[89] Guevara concluded that whatever aid the Cubans provided should be conditional, lest it turn into its opposite: allowing the "lords of the revolution" to live like princes and hold back the development of the revolution.[90]

Guerrilla Warfare without Peasant Support: Che Guevara in Bolivia

Sometime after the Congo disaster, Che Guevara anonymously returned to Cuba. Although he had failed in the Congo, he saw no reason to change the decision he had made in 1965 to resign his Cuban citizenship and government responsibilities in order to fully dedicate himself to spreading the revolution abroad.[91] With the help of the Cuban government, he began to prepare for his next expedition, which would center on Bolivia. Some have contended that Che went to Bolivia or continued to be involved in guerrilla warfare as a result of a break with Fidel Castro, or that he was abandoned by the Cuban government once he was there. The evidence to support either of these suppositions is far from conclusive.[92] It is likely that as Guevara was gradually losing out to more conservative forces in the government, a tension, rather than a break, developed between the two leaders, given that Fidel Castro now found himself pulled by two contradictory forces: on one hand, the pressure of continuing the revolutionary impulses of a still young revolution and, on the other hand, his own position as Cuba's Maximum Leader and the need to protect the interests of the nascent Cuban state and ruling class.[93] As a state leader, Fidel Castro also had to contend with the Soviet Union's considerable economic and political pressure on Cuba to refrain from getting involved in guerrilla warfare in Latin America, in contrast with its complicit role in the conduct of similar activities in Africa. Guevara resisted the Soviet Union's realpolitik pressure, insisting that spreading the revolution throughout Latin America, including Cuba, was essential to the future of "socialism."

While the notion that spread throughout the international left that Castro abandoned Guevara at some point in the Bolivian campaign is not convincing, Jorge G. Castañeda's interpretation seems more plausible. According to the Mexican academic and politician, Che alive in Cuba would have been a source of ongoing problems, tension, and dissent.[94] However, Fidel Castro did not send Che to his death in Bolivia, nor did he betray or sacrifice him. Instead, he just let history run its course, fully aware of the likely outcome. And yet again, there were reasons why Fidel Castro might have been interested along with Che in opening new guerrilla fronts in Bolivia and elsewhere in Latin America. In fact, Castro continued to support guerrilla movements on the continent even after Che's demise, although with a considerably lower profile than before the US-USSR agreement in the wake of the missile crisis of October 1962. It is true that Castro was putting at risk the Cuban state's own existence, by incurring the joint wrath of the United States and the Soviet Union. But had his guerrilla-related gamble succeeded, he might have extracted much more reliable guarantees than the precarious Soviet-American agreement of October 1962, and in the process have relieved some of the US pressure on the hard-pressed Vietnamese.[95]

For Guevara, the expedition to Bolivia was originally an attempt to establish a base from which to eventually enter Argentina, one of the most urbanized and economically developed countries in Latin America, to promote guerrilla warfare in his native country. An earlier guerrilla attempt had been made in 1964 by Jorge Ricardo Masetti, an Argentinian journalist friend of Guevara and founder of Prensa Latina, a news agency sponsored by the Cuban government. But Masetti's guerrilla group was quickly found and exterminated by Argentinian government troops.

Captured and murdered by Bolivian Rangers acting in coordination with the CIA in October 1967, Guevara did not have the opportunity to develop a serious and lengthy analysis of his experience in Bolivia similar to the one he wrote about the African experience during his lengthy stay at the Cuban embassy in Dar es Salaam, the Tanzanian capital, after having left the Congo. But he did keep an actual diary in which he registered the continuing frustrations and hardships he faced in the Bolivian jungle, including his recurring bouts of asthma and the loss of contact with another group of Cubans who had entered the country with him. Most important of all, his Bolivian diary reflects his social and political distance from the surrounding Bolivian peasantry. As with the PLA in the Congo, although for different reasons, Guevara's guerrilla group was marginal and isolated from the population around them on whose behalf they were fighting. Guevara not only failed to enlist new recruits; the peasants were informing the government about his moves, whether "through fear or deception about our aims," as he pointed out at the end of June 1967.[96] This continued to be a problem until the very end. In his final monthly summary of September 1967—shortly before he was captured and executed—Guevara remarked that, besides the greater effectiveness of the army in action, "the mass of the peasants are not helping us at all and are being turned into informers."[97]

Unlike the rebels in the Sierra Maestra, who were able to count on a strong source of support and recruitment in the extensive underground network of the July 26th movement in Cuba's urban areas, Che's expeditionary force was unable to forge an effective supportive relationship with the Bolivian left. The Bolivian Communist Party was not only proportionally much smaller than the Cuban July 26th movement, but had at best a very difficult and tense relationship with, if not an outright hostility to, Guevara's expedition. When at the end of 1966, Bolivian CP leader Mario Monje met Guevara at the guerrilla camp and demanded and was refused the leadership of the group, he broke off talks and urged the Bolivian cadres to desert.[98]

In addition, the area selected for establishing a foco base proved to be highly problematic from the standpoint of educating, recruiting, and training new recruits. In contrast with the high Bolivian altiplano, where the vast majority of the population lived but which offered little cover for guerrillas, the heavily forested and jungle regions of the east where Guevara and his group had established themselves offered good cover but little opportunity to do political work because it was sparsely populated.[99]

In any case, the question of the specific area in Bolivia where guerrilla warfare should be conducted was never satisfactorily resolved. Guevara favored the Alto Beni region of the country as the location for his future zone of operations. In fact, Régis Debray was sent there to conduct a geopolitical study of the area. But the Cubans actually in charge of the preparations had bought a 3,000-acre farm in Ñancahuazú, a different part of the country. Eventually, the plan to relocate in Alto Beni was scrapped.[100] It is hard to know whether Guevara would have been any more successful in Alto Beni or some other part of Bolivia. Moreover, General René Barrientos, the head of the Bolivian state, had far more popular and peasant support than Batista had in the Cuba of the late 1950s, and while the US government was caught unprepared with what happened in the largest of the Caribbean islands, it predictably did not let it happen in Bolivia, where it trained counterinsurgency forces to react in a rapid and decisive manner.[101]

To make things worse, the guerrilla group's multinational composition, with an entirely Cuban leadership, became the source of tensions and problems. Of the fifty guerrillas in the group, seventeen were Cuban, three Peruvian, and one East German, and the remaining twenty-nine were Bolivians (58 percent). After his experience with the disorganization and poor leadership of the Congolese rebels, Guevara had concluded he would be the top leader of any other expedition, and so it was in Bolivia. In addition, all the other officers were Cuban, with no Bolivians among them.[102] Thus, it is not surprising that in his diary entry for April 12, 1967, Guevara relates how, to allay resentment of the Cubans, he made a point of reminding his troops that the Cubans had put their bodies on the line and suffered the first rebel casualty. In the same spirit, Guevara "sought to put a halt to a tendency observed in the forward detachment of finding fault with the Cubans," a resentment that had also surfaced the previous day as one of the combatants had expressed "less and less confidence in the Cubans."[103] Unsurprisingly, the Bolivian government claimed that Bolivia was the victim of foreign intervention and set in motion a nationalist campaign against the guerrillas.[104] It is worth recalling that Fidel Castro sharply limited the number of foreigners in the 1956 *Granma* expedition, and it is not difficult to imagine that if the national composition of leadership and ranks of the rebel army operating in eastern Cuba in the years 1956–58 had been similarly foreign, it would have created a very serious political problem for the rebels, even though Cuba, lacking an indigenous population, probably had a stronger cultural identification with the rest of Latin America than did Bolivia. In sum, the Bolivian experience was another instance of Guevara's political tone-deafness and lack of political instinct, which eventually cost him his life.

The Class Politics of Guevara's Guerrilla Warfare Strategy

For Che Guevara, guerrilla warfare was the means to a successful anti-imperialist and social revolution in Latin America and its motor was the struggle of the peasant masses in pursuit of a radical agrarian reform that could only be fully realized under socialism. How did this proposition actually play out? As Guevara interpreted the experience of the Cuban Revolution, the guerrilla struggle radicalized the urban cadre as a result of their coming into contact with the peasantry and confronting its suffering. It radicalized the peasantry as a consequence of the intensified reprisals and violence inflicted on them by the army in response to peasant resistance or their refusal to collaborate with the authorities. In December 1958, for example, shortly before the rebel victory, Guevara noted in an article that the contact with the peasant masses had taught the rebels with an urban background the injustices of the existing system of rural land tenure, which convinced them of the need for a fundamental change in the agrarian property system.[105] This, however, did not fit Guevara's own political evolution, since he had been in favor of radical agrarian reform and the overthrow of capitalism long before he landed in Cuba at the end of 1956. Nor does it fit either the political evolution of the slightly more than twenty Cubans who survived the *Granma* landing. While only a few of them might have been in favor of the overthrow of capitalism at the time, all must have been in favor of agrarian reform, since it had long been the patrimony of Cuban progressive opinion, which in its most moderate form proposed the expropriation of idle lands possessed by the big latifundistas. It is even less likely that the urban cadre who joined guerrilla movements emulating the Cuban Revolution in other Latin American countries needed direct and intimate contact with their respective peasantries to develop a radical politics: almost all of them came out of radical political parties, such as the Communist Party or the left wing of popular reform parties such as Acción Democrática in Venezuela or APRA (Alianza Popular Revolucionaria Americana—American Popular Revolutionary Alliance) in Perú.[106] However, Guevara was probably correct in the sense that the Cuban rebel army members with an urban background, through their contact with the atrocious conditions of the peasantry, strengthened their commitment to a social change beyond a mere political revolution to reinstate the 1940 Constitution. As Che Guevara put it, they were enlightened by "the Cuban peasant's capacity for self-sacrifice and his unbounded nobility and loyalty."[107] But the real radicalization of the July 26th movement urban cadres, whether active in the sierra or in the llano, took place after the overthrow of the Batista dictatorship on January 1, 1959, as the radical social changes introduced by the victorious revolution confronted the increased hostility of US imperialism and the resistance of the native bourgeoisie and sections of the middle classes. After all, it was only after the overthrow of Batista that the multiclass political revolution became a social revolution strongly supported but not controlled by the working class and the peasantry.

But how did the peasants react to the sudden presence of people who, even when sharing the same language and nationality, were fundamentally outsiders and strangers in social and cultural terms? The *Granma* survivors were initially helped by the rural contacts provided to them through the July 26th movement networks in nearby towns and cities, such as those that Celia Sánchez, who was to become Fidel Castro's principal aide and advisor, provided to Fidel Castro's group. Yet the Cuban rebels were beset by the reality of peasant informers and traitors, such as the infamous Eutímio Guerra, who was executed shortly after he was discovered to be informing for and collaborating with the Cuban Army.[108]

The pressure of the government's armed forces that flooded the areas where the rebels operated was compounded by the effect it had in encouraging peasant spying and informing. However, as Guevara observed, if the peasants became convinced that the army would not succeed in eradicating the insurgency—in other words, that the government was not winning, but might still be capable of wiping out the peasants' homes, crops, and families—they in turn might then decide to take refuge with the guerrillas.[109] However, this calculus aside, the peasants' sympathy toward or alienation from the government must have played a critical role in determining which side to ultimately support. Thus, in the very different case of Bolivia, when the peasants in the area where Guevara and his companions operated seemed to at least have given the benefit of the doubt to the government, the problem of informers seemed to have been much more severe than in Cuba, especially shortly before Che was captured and executed in October 1967.[110] Earlier, in his "Summary of the Month" at the end of April 1967 (the guerrilla campaign had begun in November 1966), Guevara had already underscored the distance and alienation between his group and the local peasantry, noting that not a single peasant had yet been recruited and that "our peasant base still needs to be developed, although it appears that through planned terror we can obtain the neutrality of most; support will come later."[111] It is revealing that Guevara and his comrades began to get a better reception among those peasants with whom they had developed a personal rather than merely political relationship over time in the area in which they operated.[112]

In contradiction to his tenet that the peasantry was the motor of the revolution, the guerrilla warfare strategy envisaged by Guevara entailed an "outside" and "from above" relationship to the peasantry. While discussing his thoughts on that topic, he cited a fragment from the Second Declaration of Havana, proclaimed on February 4, 1962, which includes the observation that "the peasantry is a class which, because of the ignorance in which it has been kept and the isolation in which it lives, requires the revolutionary and the political leadership of the working class and the revolutionary intellectuals," the leadership being the Communist Party.[113] Following Guevara's logic, Héctor Béjar, the Peruvian guerrilla leader active in his country, when talking about his fundamental assumptions and expectations about the role of the peasantry in his guerrilla strategy, assigned them the role of supporting cast rather than of lead actor. When Béjar asked himself if the guerrillas had peasant support, he answered:

> If by that is meant a general and well-elaborated theoretical conviction and massive and well-organized aid, then evidently we did not. To ask for that kind of support would be to deal with metaphysics, not realities. If, however, by peasant support we mean the collaboration of most of the people, originating in their certainty that we were there to defend them, then we did have it and, moreover, it surpassed anything we had expected.[114]

The great majority of the Cuban peasantry became radicalized after the victory of the Cuban Revolution on January 1, 1959. They became enthusiastic supporters of the revolution especially around the time of the first Agrarian Reform, approved in May 1959, a radical but not collectivist law, which granted the land to those who worked it and "resolved" the question of compensation by promising twenty-year bonds, a promise that was never really enforced. The Agrarian Reform law mentioned the formation of cooperatives almost as an afterthought. Later on, however, the state took over the overwhelming majority of the land and imposed bureaucratic and inefficient state farms in the Soviet mold, which became, for many decades, the predominant form of rural property in Cuba. Yet, the peasantry continued to support the government because its standard of living—in terms of guaranteed employment, education, health, and social mobility (much of this through migration to the cities)—considerably improved, at least during the thirty years previous to the Special Period brought about by the collapse of the USSR and the Soviet bloc in the late 1980s and early 1990s. The fact that most people working the land were rural workers rather than peasants facilitated the government's takeover of the land since these rural workers were much more interested in improving their standard of living than on the acquisition of land as such. In any case, the policies regarding the land were not made by former peasant rebels. The revolutionary government remained under the control of the urban, and overwhelmingly white, rebel leadership. Very few of the peasants who joined the rebel army played major leadership, policy-making roles in the revolutionary government.

Guerrilla Warfare and the Working Class

Was guerrilla warfare as a military strategy inherently incompatible with an orientation to the working class? A close analysis will show that a guerrilla strategy is compatible with many different political ideologies and class commitments.[115] Even the existence of a "foco," meaning a usually limited geographical area where rebels are able to establish military and political control, does not in itself determine its class or political orientation. Thus, a large and well-organized labor or multi-class urban movement in a prerevolutionary period might have its own fighting units and military commands both in urban and rural areas. A foco could also conceivably act as a secure location from which support for urban and especially working-class oriented activities could be launched and as a safe place where the greatly endangered activists from the cities could take shelter (as in fact commonly occurred in the Sierra Maestra in 1957 and 1958).[116] Last but not least, a foco with an urban working-class orientation could play an important psychological role as a beacon of hope, showing that the army and the government are not invincible and can be defeated.

It is important to emphasize that, on the eve of the Cuban Revolution, the Cuban working class was hardly unimportant, even though it did not have its own independent unions or organizations. By the early 1950s, Cuba had become a substantially urbanized society. The census of 1953 counted 5.8 million people on the island, with 57 percent being urban and 43 percent rural. An analysis of the figures provided by the US Department of Commerce, on the basis of the same census, classified 22.7 percent of the Cuban labor force under the category of craftsmen, foremen, and operatives, 7.2 percent as clerical workers, and 6.2 percent as sales workers. Service workers, except private household employees, constituted 4.2 percent and private household workers 4.0 percent of the labor force. These categories show the urban working class as having constituted 44.3 percent of the labor force and farm laborers (including unpaid family workers) as 28.8 percent of the labor force, which could be seen as a rough approximation of the rural working class. This class grouping was more than twice the size of the 11.3 percent of the labor force that was classified as farmers and ranchers, a rural petty bourgeoisie that could nevertheless be very poor.[117] Union density, although organized in mostly bureaucratic and corrupt unions, was quite high, with some one million members out of a labor force of approximately two million workers. It is true that there was not much of a working class or much economic development in the Congo except for Katanga, but the Bolivian working class centered on the tin miners was a major force that had played a central role in the revolution of 1952, which led to a significant agrarian reform and the nationalization of the mines.

Nevertheless, the failed April 1958 strike in Cuba led to the fateful decision of the sierra leadership to relegate working-class action in the cities to a subordinate and supporting role, for which Guevara was the most articulate spokesperson. In his treatise on guerrilla warfare published in 1960, Guevara insisted that in the underdeveloped Americas, the countryside was the central area for armed fighting, a strategy that he intended to take to an extreme and even absurd length by extending it to his native country of Argentina, one of the most urbanized and economically developed in Latin America, with a long tradition of urban working-class struggle.

Guevara, like most Maoists, seemed to have assumed that revolutionary militancy was directly proportional to the degree of misery experienced by a group or class. He theorized that the industrial workers "who, under present conditions in the Congo, are privileged in their exploitation," would only join the revolution at a later stage, closing "ranks with the guerrilla movement, as a result of the catalyzing effect of armed activity."[118] Guevara's notion of "privileged exploitation" is very problematic. Quite aside from being alien to classical Marxism, it suggests a notion of "privilege" not on the basis of a group demonstrably being favored through its clear oppression or exploitation of others, but instead on being quantitatively less exploited (and oppressed) than other groups. But his linking militancy with the degree of suffering and misery was in the case of Cuba historically incorrect: among the most militant opponents of the Batista dictatorship were the unions of bank and electricity workers, among the best paid workers in the country.

Guevara sometimes contradicted his own theory regarding the role of class in guerrilla warfare by positing the conflict between exploiting and exploited nations as the principal contradiction of the epoch.[119] It is not at all clear if he attempted to integrate this view with his peasant-centered guerrilla strategy. His alternative perspective based on the "exploiting/exploited nation" dynamics could have led to a very different and much more conservative strategy of alliances with the native progressive bourgeoisie and related strata. Guevara, however, was sometimes able to resolve such contradictions by changing the usual meaning of terms. Thus, for example, he had managed to resolve the apparent contradiction of his support for the worker-peasant alliance with his dim view of the potentialities of the working class by reformulating it as an "alliance of the highly backward peasantry" not with the real flesh-and-blood working class, but with the "*ideology* of the proletariat," which in fact meant the ideology of the Communist Party.[120]

It was in Bolivia that Guevara's theory, strategy, and tactics regarding the working class were put to the test seriously. He was already in that country with his guerrilla force when the army massacred the miners of the Siglo XX mines, leaving many of them dead and wounded.

In reaction, Guevara issued a communiqué warning the miners to refrain from following the "false apostles of mass struggle," arguing that "against modern instruments of destruction, barricades, however well constructed, are of no avail." In underdeveloped countries such as Bolivia, Guevara insisted, with a large peasant base and a large territory, the mass struggle should revolve around a small, mobile guerrilla vanguard "firmly based among the people." As the guerrilla force acquired strength against the army, it would increase the masses' revolutionary fervor, leading to a revolutionary situation. That was when, Guevara said, "state power will be toppled in a single well-aimed and well-timed blow." While Guevara pointed out that he was not calling for total inactivity and urged the workers to continue to bring pressure against the government, since they were engaged in a class struggle with unlimited fronts, the main point of his communiqué was to call on them to join the guerrillas. According to Guevara, this was the place where the worker–peasant alliance could be rebuilt to turn defeat into victory.[121] In light of the serious defeat the miners suffered at the hands of the Bolivian army, Guevara could have instead suggested alternative tactics to avoid such lethal confrontations, while continuing the struggle at the workplace and communities where the miners worked and lived. Instead, he made the highly unrealistic proposal of asking the miners to abandon their jobs, families, and communities to move elsewhere to join his guerrilla group, a call that even under the best circumstances, only a few miners were likely to heed. It is significant that, beyond abandoning their families and mines to join a guerrilla struggle, the miners were being asked to join a group with a military command structure, hierarchy, and discipline that by definition excluded democratic political debate and discussion, hardly the vehicle for the self-emancipation of the working class that Marx and Engels had politically advocated and worked to build.

Chapter Three

Che Guevara in Power

It is striking that Che Guevara's status as an international icon is almost entirely based on his militant activities and writings as an international guerrilla fighter in Cuba, the Congo, and Bolivia. Yet, one could make a strong argument that his most important and consequential political legacy was the major role he played as one of the principal leaders of the Cuban Revolution, building a new socioeconomic and political system on the island, thus shaping the future of Cuba for generations to come.

When Batista was overthrown on January 1, 1959, Fidel Castro had already emerged as the dominant leader of the July 26th revolutionary movement. Right behind him, Che Guevara was, along with Camilo Cienfuegos and Raúl Castro, one of the three other principal leaders of the rebel army, and certainly the most politically and culturally sophisticated of the three. Although a special revolutionary law had made Guevara a citizen with the same rights as a native Cuban, this did not entirely remove the subtle but real political disadvantage of his being a foreigner. His cold and distant personality, in some ways similar to Raúl Castro's, encouraged a great deal of popular respect and even awe, but not love, and certainly not the popular adoration bestowed on Fidel Castro and Camilo Cienfuegos. With his slight physical resemblance to popular representations of Jesus Christ and Camilo's urban working-class background,

Cienfuegos represented to the Cuban people the ideal virtues of a warm demeanor, good humor, and good looks.

Political Tendencies in the Early Period of the Revolution

Che Guevara's political role in the early stages of the victorious revolution can be properly understood only in the context of the llano-sierra political division that I analyzed in the previous chapter and the transformation it went through after the revolutionary victory into a partly public and partly hidden struggle among political tendencies fighting over the fate of the Cuban Revolution. These conflicting tendencies included the July 26th movement, other organizations such as the PSP and the DR, and unaffiliated individuals. Although the issues in dispute and the number of personalities and tendencies involved grew after the victory of January 1, 1959, there was a significant continuity with the conflicts and alignments of the preceding period.

The Liberals

The liberal tendency was represented by a number of people, some active in the July 26th movement against Batista, who did not directly participate in the sierra-llano dispute but were connected to civil society organizations that supported the new revolutionary government. Many of them became ministers in the cabinet installed immediately after Batista was overthrown. They all shared to various degrees a desire to reform the Cuban political and socioeconomic system without challenging its capitalist foundation, while still favoring a substantial degree of state intervention. Critical of US foreign policy but not anti-imperialists, these liberals hoped for an alliance with the United States on the basis of a reformed and more respectful US attitude to Cuban sovereignty. They also supported agrarian reform that would have emphasized the expropriation of idle lands and the compensation required by the Constitution of 1940, although they mostly accepted the more radical measures of the agrarian reform law approved in May 1959, provided that the law's inclusion of cooperatives did not lead to far more drastic measures such as the wholesale nationalization of agriculture. The liberals would have liked to see the "arbitrary" administration of the law by the rebel army replaced by the rule of law administered by a re-formed judicial system. They firmly supported the militant Keynesian pol-icies adopted by Fidel Castro's government in the early part of 1959, which involved a partial fiscal amnesty—in return for the prompt payment of the remaining overdue tax contributions—that brought an enormous amount of money into the Cuban treasury. With these funds, the Cuban govern-ment financed a massive program of public works to employ the hundreds of thousands of idled sugar workers after the short sugar season was over. Liberals such as Felipe Pazos, a well-known economist and the head of the National Bank of Cuba; Manuel Ray, a civil engineer who had been active in the urban underground, as minister of public works; and Rufo López Fresquet, an economist and minister of the treasury, were directly involved in administering this policy. The government liberals were also supportive of the early government campaign urging people to buy products made in Cuba, a measure welcomed by Cuban industrialists, which had the unan-ticipated and for them unwelcome result of contributing to the revival of the anti-imperialist mood that had been dormant on the island during the previous twenty years. Other liberals in the government included Elena Mederos, a pioneering social worker who was appointed minister of social work; Manuel Urrutia Lleó, a former provincial judge (known for hav-ing voted to absolve rebels appearing before his court during the struggle against Batista), who served as president until July 1959; and the more conservative José Miró Cardona, the former head of the Bar Association, who functioned for six weeks as prime minister until Fidel Castro took over the position in February 1959.

At the time of the revolutionary victory, the liberal political current had a number of political points in its favor. The traditional right in Cuba was weak and somewhat discredited because of its close associ-ation with the conservative Catholic and pro-Spanish daily *Diario de la Marina*, which had opposed Cuban independence and supported Franco's forces in the Spanish Civil War. Very few of the government liberals had previously occupied important governmental positions and were therefore untainted by the reality or suspicion of corruption. Since many of them had connections with civil society, they had a potential social base in the important Cuban middle classes (some public employ-ees, professionals, and small businesspeople among others). Yet, they were unable to mobilize and capitalize on that potentially important source of support because along with practically all other political forces in Cuban society, by 1959 they had become subordinated to the imposing figure of Fidel Castro. An indication of their inability to remain independent and grow politically was the formal dissolution of the primarily middle-class Movimiento de Resistencia Cívica (Movement of Civic Resistance) that had actively collaborated with the revolutionaries of the July 26th movement during the struggle against the Batista dictatorship in February 1959.

The Nationalist Anti-Imperialist Revolutionaries

An important non-Communist, nationalist, anti-imperialist current of revolutionaries had functioned primarily within the amorphous and weakly organized July 26th movement and had distinguished themselves in the struggle against the Batista dictatorship mostly in the llano (the urban underground). They constituted, in the words of Paco Ignacio Taibo II, Guevara's sympathetic Mexican biographer, a left-wing sector that combined "anti-imperialism with a strong critique of the Communists, who [were] considered to be conservative and sectarian."[1] Among these was Carlos Franqui, a former Communist who ran Radio Rebelde in the sierra and later became the editor of *Revolución*, the newspaper of the July 26th movement; David Salvador, also a former Communist, who had been a leader of the sugar workers in eastern Cuba and became, after the victory of the revolution, the head of the CTC (Confederación de Trabajadores de Cuba, Confederation of Cuban Workers); and Faustino Pérez, Marcelo Fernández, and Enrique Oltuski, all major leaders of the July 26th movement urban underground. One of the most important contributions of this group was its strong nationalist anti-imperialism. David Salvador grabbed headlines in the United States and Latin America when, in March 1959, he publicly interrupted a speech by visiting liberal Costa Rican leader José Figueres and strongly criticized his pro-US Cold War stand. This was one of the early signals that the Cuban Revolution was going to follow a different path from the liberal reform road taken by previously successful movements against Latin American dictatorships in countries such as Venezuela. *Revolución*, with a large and growing circulation, became the principal mass press organ conveying the renewed Cuban anti-imperialist nationalism. *Revolución* engaged in frequent polemics with the right-wing press such as *Diario de la Marina*, and less often with the liberal *Prensa Libre* and with the Communist *Hoy*, which assiduously tried to channel the resurgent Cuban anti-imperialism into the pro-Soviet mold.

On more than one occasion, one of *Revolución*'s editorialists (probably Marcelo Fernández, the national coordinator of the July 26th movement) wrote about the need for building a democratically controlled revolutionary organization, which at that time clearly meant excluding the PSP, the old Communist Party, a position that was anathema to people like Guevara and Raúl Castro, who were then pushing hard for a policy of unity with the Communists.[2] *Revolución* also sponsored one of the most interesting and independent left-wing literary and cultural supplements in Latin America, the weekly *Lunes de Revolución*, edited by Guillermo Cabrera Infante, a film critic who later became an internationally famous writer. *Lunes*, which had a mass circulation, not only published the work of several young Cuban writers and poets such as Antón Arrufat, Pablo Armando Fernández, and Heberto Padilla, but also a wide variety of non-Communist left-wing international authors, such as Jean-Paul Sartre and Simone de Beauvoir. *Lunes* was suppressed shortly after Fidel Castro's announcement of his cultural policy, which he summarized with the slogan "Inside the revolution, everything; outside the revolution, nothing" in 1961.[3] Castro conveniently ignored the key question of who decided what was "inside the revolution."

But it was on the trade union front that these independent revolutionaries, who sometimes called themselves "humanist," left their biggest mark.[4] Shortly after Batista fled the country, union halls throughout the island were taken over by revolutionary trade unionists. While those associated with the July 26th movement were the most numerous and influential among them, many were part of the anti-imperialist nationalist tendency. All the "Mujalista" labor leaders—supporters of Eusebio Mujal, head of the official trade unions under Batista, who had collaborated with the Batista dictatorship—were purged, and the new revolutionary union leaders placed a great deal of emphasis on the union democracy that had been so thoroughly crushed under "Mujalismo." A vigorous unionizing campaign was immediately launched with the support of the revolutionary government and was very successful. This was followed, in spring 1959, by elections in every single local union in the country, and these were in turn followed by elections at the regional and national level, when many of those who had taken over the unions were then elected to their posts. These elections turned out to be the most important exercise in autonomous grassroots democracy of the revolutionary period. The candidates associated with the July 26th movement emerged as the overwhelming winners. Communists only managed to obtain some 10 percent of the union posts, although it is important to note that some of the elected July 26th movement candidates had Communist sympathies. The outcomes of the spring elections were remarkably consistent with the results of a union survey the PSP had conducted in 1956 showing that of the two thousand local unions in the country, those led by Communists and those willing to work with them constituted only 15 percent.[5]

However, as was the case with the liberals, the power of the nationalist anti-imperialists was very limited by their dependence on Fidel Castro. After all, *Revolución,* as the official organ of the July 26th movement, was ultimately controlled by Fidel Castro, and, to a considerable extent, the Cuban workers voted for the July 26th movement candidates because they saw them as Fidel Castro's followers.

The Che Guevara–Raúl Castro–PSP Alliance

When Che Guevara arrived in Havana after the revolution's victory, Fidel Castro appointed him as the head of the important military installation at La Cabaña, an old Spanish fortress sitting on the east side of Havana Bay right behind the Morro Castle at the bay's opening. Although Guevara tried, and was perhaps pressured by Fidel Castro, to lower his public profile in the early days of the revolution in order to avoid a premature airing of the issue of Communism, his political sympathies were clear.[6] As early as January 27, 1959, he publicly expressed his political leanings in a speech, "Social Ideas of the Rebel Army," to the Sociedad Nuestro Tiempo, the most important cultural PSP front organization.[7] When confronted by a hostile press, he tried to walk a difficult line, neither denying his politics nor compromising a government of which he was a major leader with positions that Fidel Castro, at least at this time, did not (and could not) endorse. Thus, when an interviewer in the television program *Telemundo Pregunta* asked him on April 29, 1959, "Are you a communist?" Guevara responded: "I have been asked that question very often and I do not have to answer it because the facts speak for themselves. If you think that what we do for the people is communism, then we are communists; if you ask me if I am member of the Partido Socialista Popular, then I would answer no."[8] At the same time, however, Raúl Castro and Che Guevara were organizing an alliance with the PSP based on what they called the need for "revolutionary unity." This strategic line was first put forward by the PSP, seconded by Raúl Castro and Che Guevara, and eventually endorsed by Fidel Castro many months later in fall 1959. The initial programmatic basis for this "unity" was rather vague, but the organizational meaning of the term clearly involved the collaboration of the PSP with those wings of the July 26th movement and other revolutionary organizations that, although not necessarily admirers of the PSP, were willing to refrain from criticizing or opposing PSP politics. In practice, "unity" also came to mean that the PSP and its allies could freely criticize others within the revolutionary camp but that if those others, whether the liberals or the nationalist anti-imperialists, criticized the PSP, they were to be labeled as "divisive" anti-Communists. The PSP was allowed to expound its version of Communist politics, but the people who opposed the party, whether from a right-wing or left-wing perspective, were officially defined as part of a right-wing "anti-Communist" amalgam.[9]

The PSP had clearly gained some distinct advantages from its alliance with Raúl Castro and Che Guevara. Although both of these leaders enjoyed a great deal of prestige, their power and autonomy were circumscribed by their dependence on Fidel Castro in a way that did not apply to the PSP. While they had to be careful in their pronouncements because they represented the government, the PSP had much more freedom to propound its politics and was able to provide the only systematic explanation of events to its members and to the radicalized Fidelistas. The PSP exploited its ideological monopoly. At this early stage of the revolution, it became the one significant political force with a systematic political methodology speaking in the name of Marxism and socialism.[10]

The "unity" approach bore fruit by the first half of 1959. An important indicator of its success occurred in the trade unions. Although the strength of the PSP in the trade unions was very limited, the PSP-influenced "unity" union slates did somewhat better and became the dominant force in a handful of the thirty-three "industrial federations," including the textile, restaurant, and transport workers unions. They had also been elected in a number of locals of other federations that represented sugar, tobacco, and maritime workers.[11] However, in overall terms, they still remained a relatively small minority in the union movement. But their most important accomplishment was winning over a significant number of rebel army majors who became closely identified with the "unity" line, including Majors Augusto Martínez Sánchez, William Gálvez, Demetrio Montseny (Villa), Manuel Piñeiro, and Faure Chomón from the Directorio Revolucionario.[12]

While making some progress on the open political front, the Che Guevara–Raúl Castro–PSP alliance was also making a different and much greater progress beneath the surface within the political and government machinery. On January 13, just a few days after having taken charge of La Cabaña fortress, Che inaugurated an "Academia Militar-Cultural" (Military-Cultural Academy) to teach basic literacy and raise the cultural and political awareness of the army garrison. He banned cockfighting and instead organized chess classes, an equestrian team, sports events, art exhibits, concerts, and theater productions at La Cabaña. He also founded a local newspaper to serve the fortress and soon helped to found *Verde Olivo*, which became the political hard-line newspaper of the armed forces. Soon after, Che discreetly placed the academy under the direction of Armando Acosta, a PSP cadre who had been his political commissar in central Cuba in the final stages of the struggle against Batista.[13]

Following the directives of Fidel Castro, Che was also secretly meeting with Raúl Castro—who went back and forth from Santiago de Cuba to Havana—and with Camilo Cienfuegos, Ramiro Valdés, and Víctor Pina, a member of the PSP, to create a new state security apparatus. The G-2, later known as Seguridad del Estado, was placed in the hands of Ramiro Valdés, a founding member of the July 26th movement and Che's deputy during the war against Batista's army. Osvaldo Sánchez, a member of the PSP's Politburo and head of its "Military Committee," became Valdés's second in command.[14]

In early 1959, the Soviet government decided to offer help to the PSP and allies, despite its low profile and the limited support it had lent to the Cuban revolutionary process. As a result, in March 1959, a PSP representative met with the chief of staff of the Soviet armed forces, Marshall V. Sokolovsky, to discuss further relations between the two armed services.[15] Most important, in April 1959, Raúl Castro sent

Lázaro Peña, one of the most important PSP leaders, to Moscow to request that Spanish Communists who had graduated from the Soviet military academy come to help the Cuban army organize intelligence work and other matters. While Fidel Castro was visiting the United States, Khrushchev's presidium approved Raúl Castro's request on April 23, and two officers of Spanish origin were immediately sent to Cuba. Fifteen others joined them a short time later. The Soviets paid for the officers' salaries and expenses.[16] Meanwhile, Sokolovsky began to raise with a PSP representative the possibility of training Cuba's pilots and inquired about the party's goals for the armed forces.[17]

Che Guevara experienced some health problems during this period. On March 4, he was diagnosed with a pulmonary infection and, under doctor's orders, he and his wife, Aleida, moved to a villa at nearby Tarará Beach. In Tarará, the work to prepare the agrarian reform law and to establish INRA (Instituto Nacional de Reforma Agraria – National Institute for Agrarian Reform) intensified. A secret agrarian reform task force headed by the geographer Antonio Nuñez Jiménez met nightly at Che's house. Besides Nuñez Jiménez, who was friendly with the PSP, the task force included Che, Alfredo Guevara (an old Communist friend of Fidel), Pedro Miret, Vilma Espín (Raúl Castro's new wife), and two senior PSP advisors. No one associated with the nationalist anti-imperialist tendency was invited to these meetings. As far as the government liberals were concerned, absolute secrecy was maintained from Manuel Urrutia, the president, and from his cabinet. Humberto Sorí-Marín, the official minister of agriculture and a liberal who had drafted the moderate agrarian reform law that the rebels had approved in the Sierra in 1958, was completely kept out of the process to draft the new law.[18] Since Fidel Castro was aware of and occasionally attended these meetings, the Tarará conclaves signified a major victory for the Che Guevara–Raúl Castro–PSP alliance.

Until fall 1959, Fidel Castro publicly appeared to remain above the fray. For the most part, he abstained from participating in the open conflicts within the revolutionary camp, reserving for himself the role of ultimate arbiter. This made it easier for him to combat one enemy at a time and postpone certain major conflicts, while taking careful account of the relations of social and political forces. Unlike Raúl and Che Guevara, he avoided a premature commitment to a political course that could have undermined his hold on power.[19] While Fidel Castro may have been ready to preside over a system that was not Communist, Che Guevara would have split with Fidel and probably left the country, and Raúl Castro would have probably gone into opposition, in alliance with the PSP, if Cuba had not embraced Communism.

Notwithstanding Che Guevara and Raúl Castro's major influence on Cuban events, Fidel Castro had political designs that he shared with no one. Although he wanted to make a radical revolution, he left it to historical circumstances, the existing relation of forces and tactical possibilities, to determine specifically what kind of revolution it would be, while making sure all along that he remained in control. Although he did not necessarily foresee becoming a part of the Soviet bloc, he did not preclude it. His considerable political talents were eminently tactical. He knew how to advance his agenda in a certain general but unspecified leftist political direction by taking advantage of particular political conjunctures and the existing relationship of social and political forces. Viewed in a comparative perspective, had he turned in a different political direction, he would not have been the first national leader to collaborate with the local Communists and with the Soviet Union to eventually take an alternative political road or, as in the case of Chiang Kai Shek in China, to totally turn against them.

The secret meetings at Tarará to draft the radical agrarian reform law that was approved in May 1959 have led authors such as Tad Szulc, who covered Cuba for the *New York Times* in the late 1950s and early 1960s, to conclude that the eventual Communist outcome of the Cuban Revolution resulted from a conscious plan developed by Castro and his close associates in collaboration with the leadership of the PSP prior to Batista's overthrow on January 1, 1959.[20] This conspiratorial theory is still being put forward by the US and Cuban right wing, much as liberals and part of the left keep on propounding the view that the island nation went Communist mainly because the United States pushed Castro's Cuba into the arms of the Soviet Union.

The Tarará meetings and the development of the intelligence and military apparatus obviously point to the existence of an active collaboration between Fidel Castro and several important leaders in the government such as Che Guevara and Raúl Castro with the PSP and even with the Soviet Union. The PSP, a relatively small but well organized and politically experienced apparatus, was providing Fidel Castro with an effective tool to realize his aims against the government liberals, while for the time being Fidel Castro ignored the nationalist anti-imperialists whose principled objections to Communism made them, from his point of view, unreliable supporters and allies. Fidel Castro took a risk in granting the PSP a growing organizational power. And indeed, they became an important problem that Fidel Castro was strong and skillful enough to overcome without much cost to the stability of the new regime in the successful fight against "sectarianism" personified in Aníbal Escalante, one of the most sectarian Communist leaders, in 1962. But none of this means that Fidel had already decided by March 1959, much less by 1958, as Szulc claimed, to establish Communism on the island. Viewed in its totality, the evidence suggests that a political alliance with the Soviet Union did not happen until fall 1959. Had there been such a clear decision by Fidel Castro in early 1959, Raúl Castro would have never put in doubt his brother's political intentions during his visit to the United States in April 1959 at the invitation of the American Society of Newspaper Editors. During that trip, Fidel Castro softened his critical tone toward the United States and disassociated himself from Communism. This alarmed Raúl, who telephoned Fidel and told him that there was talk at home that the Yankees were "seducing" him. Indignant, Fidel rejected his younger brother's insinuations.[21] According to declassified Soviet documents, Raúl Castro briefly considered splitting the rebel movement to convince his brother that he could not govern without the Communists. In addition, until the fall, Fidel Castro allowed the newspaper *Revolución* (the official organ of the July 26th movement, a paper whose offices he regularly visited), to engage in polemics with the PSP, countering the "unity" line. Earlier, in spring 1959, elections had been carried out in every union local in the country without any interference from Fidel Castro, which predictably resulted in a very clear defeat for the PSP and its allies. Perhaps as a way to relieve some of the pressure from the Guevara–Raúl Castro–PSP alliance, Fidel Castro sent Guevara on a very long diplomatic tour of Asia and Africa that effectively took him out of decision-making circles for practically the entire summer of 1959. Finally, throughout the whole period from January to September 1959, neither the PSP nor the Soviet Union behaved in a way that suggested they had reached an agreement with Fidel Castro but rather were still trying to influence and win him over.[22]

The Turn Toward an Alliance with the Soviet Union and the PSP

A series of events took place between September and November 1959 that indicated that Fidel Castro had opted for an alliance, and not simply an ad hoc collaboration, with the Soviet Union and the PSP. This was preceded in the summer months by an active government campaign against anti-Communist politics within the revolutionary camp. In one of the worst examples of Fidel Castro's manipulative politics, liberal president Manuel Urrutia was forced to resign in July 1959.[23] Most significantly, Euclides Vázquez Candela, the non-Communist but radical chief theoretician of *Revolución*, put an end to the recurring debates with the PSP in September 1959 but accused the party of trying to portray the July 26th movement as merely a provisional formation to prevent it from becoming a permanent organization. Vázquez Candela reiterated the need for such an organization and went on to specify the nature of his objections to the PSP's politics:

> To be a communist plain and simple is a way of confronting reality like many others and as such not at all shameful in itself. . . . To be a communist of a party of the Cominform is already, without doubt, to adopt a type of Marxism compromised with the interests and demands of a metropolis in which one blindly trusts in . . . the universal establishment of socialism. The open belligerence against these two forms of conduct and living is not at the center of our struggle. We have our own position, and we will defend it with the same right that all revolutions have defended their way of facing the restructuring of the society in which they must act.[24]

On October 1, Aleksandr Alekseev arrived in Havana to act as the Soviet Union's unofficial envoy to the Cuban revolutionary leadership, and the first leader he asked to meet was Che Guevara.[25] Later in October, former schoolteacher and rebel army major Huber Matos resigned in protest over the growing Communist influence in the armed forces. Fidel Castro did not respond by owning up to socialism and Communism, although, as we saw above, he had been attacking anti-Communism as divisive at least since he forced President Urrutia to resign. In a furious reaction, the revolutionary leader accused Matos of treason and had him sentenced to twenty years in prison, which he served in its entirety, in a show trial in which no conspiracy or incitement to violence on Matos's part was ever proved. The announcement of Matos's trial provoked an unpublicized split in the government. Faustino Pérez and Enrique Oltuski, who belonged to the nationalist, anti-imperialist wing, and Manuel Ray, one of the still surviving liberals in the cabinet, objected to the Matos trial. Pérez, Oltuski, and Ray maintained that Matos had separated himself from the revolution but had not committed an act of treason. Fidel Castro insisted that Matos should go to prison and asked for the resignation of the dissenting cabinet members. Che Guevara, perhaps troubled by Fidel Castro's abusive tone and impressed by the dignified response of Enrique Oltuski, Faustino Pérez, and Manuel Ray, argued that since they had the courage to risk their lives in order to stick to their opinions, they should continue in their posts.[26] Oltuski temporarily remained as minister of communications, but the other two left the government in November and were replaced by people with similar politics to Raúl Castro and Che Guevara.[27] In October, another liberal, Felipe Pazos, who had also objected to the trial of Huber Matos, resigned as president of the National Bank of Cuba (the equivalent of the Federal Reserve in the United States) and was replaced by Che Guevara. In a sign of irreverence, he signed the new peso bills simply with his nickname.

However, the most important sign that Fidel Castro and his government had made a significant turn in its policies and alignments was the tenth trade union congress that took place in November 1959. The election of delegates to the congress in early November produced very similar results to those of the spring elections. Once the congress began, it was clear that the Communist delegation would take a drubbing and be excluded from the leadership bodies of the trade union confederation. At this point, Fidel Castro personally intervened and a different leadership slate was approved. While well-known Communists were kept off the slate, the so-called unitarian elements of the July 26th movement who were friendly to the Communists and were led by Jesús Soto were given a predominant role.

After the Congress concluded, the Labor Ministry, under Fidel Castro's control, assisted by the Communist union leaders and the unitarian elements friendly to them, began to purge a large number of trade union leaders who had resisted Communist influence. This process was carried out by means of commissions and carefully staged and controlled union meetings instead of new elections. About 50 percent of the labor leaders, most of whom belonged to the July 26th movement and had been freely elected in the spring 1959 local and national union elections, were removed. Many were persecuted and jailed as well. Veteran PSP cadres and their "unitarian" collaborators took over these leadership positions. The government's anti-imperialism and especially the significant material improvements enjoyed by the working class and the majority of the Cuban people had provided Castro and his government such great support in 1959 and 1960 that any labor leader they chose could have been easily removed from office had there been new elections; any slate of candidates supported by Castro and his government would have undoubtedly won.[28] However, from the Cuban leader's long-term perspective, new elections would have allowed the unions to retain their autonomy. The purges allowed the unions to be turned into his policy tools at a time when he had begun to move politically toward the Soviet Union and the Cuban Communists. In 1961, less than two years after the fateful tenth congress of the union confederation, the government approved new legislation that brought the nature and function of Cuban trade unions into alignment with those of the Soviet bloc. The new functions were to help production, to promote efficiency and expansion of social and public services, to improve the administration of all sectors of the economy, and to carry out political education.[29]

The eleventh congress of the union confederation that took place in November 1961 was completely different from the tenth congress of November 1959. Unanimity had now replaced controversy and all leaders were elected by acclamation. Not surprisingly, the old Stalinist leader Lázaro Peña regained the position of secretary general, which he had last held in the 1940s under Batista. Of the seventeen national union leaders elected in 1959, only five remained in the twelve-member leadership group "elected" at the conclusion of the congress. The new leadership agreed to give up some gains that Cuban workers had obtained even before the revolution. Yet, even after replacing the duly elected union leadership and eliminating union autonomy, it would take a while to eliminate the militancy of Cuban workers. Thus, in June 1960, when he was the head of the industrial department of the National Institute of Agrarian Reform (he would become minister of industry in 1961), Che Guevara insisted that it was "necessary to change the way of thinking of labor union leaders. Their function is not to shout louder than the boss or to impose absurd measures within the production system such as getting wages for people that do not work. If a worker gets pay without earning it, he conspires against the nation and against himself."[30] In this and other instances, Che Guevara, as a leader of the government, was asking the workers to comply with the government's new rationalized work environment and, much more important, to give up their union's organizational independence. By and large, however, workers implicitly accepted the new labor order in exchange for the social and economic gains they had achieved under the regime and the new nationalist anti-imperialist solidarity they shared with the revolutionary leaders.

Che Guevara, Strikes, and Workers' Representation at the Workplace

It is not surprising then that Che Guevara did not look kindly on the workers' right to strike. In June 1960, he declared that it would be inadmissible and nothing less than the beginning of the end for the revolution for the workers to have to go on strike just because the employer state adopted an "intransigent and absurd position that forced the workers to strike."[31] By June 1961, as minister of industry, Ernesto Che Guevara put forward the unequivocal notion that "the Cuban workers have to get used to living in a collectivist regime and therefore cannot strike."[32] Here Guevara was putting in his own "collectivist" words the notion that since the state was a workers' state, there could not be a real difference of interests between the workers and the state, ignoring the persistence of class differences, let alone the hierarchical division of labor, under socialism. In later years, after Che had resigned his government positions and renounced his Cuban citizenship and was preparing to go to the Congo, he privately admitted in his *Apuntes*, published forty years later, that while there should be no unions under socialism because there is no class exploitation, unions are necessary at the level of the local workplace to avoid a number of potential abuses.[33] However, one might wonder what practical difference Guevara's new attitude would have made since he made clear in the same text his opposition to any adversarial bargaining relationship between the workers and the employer state, which by Guevara's definition is identical to the workers' vanguard.[34] In light of his overall monolithic conception of socialism that ignored the hierarchical division of labor and ruled out any conflict of interests other than the class interests that were being eliminated, Guevara could not conceive of the specific functions that unions could fulfill in a socialist society.

Guevara was no more able to understand and grapple with the need for democratic participation and decision-making at the micro level of the workplace than he did at the macro level, as we shall see below in the discussion of his principal work *Socialism and Man in Cuba*. As an undoubtedly highly intelligent person, he acknowledged that it was not the same thing to direct a large factory and to be a worker in that factory, since "workers and administrators even today see problems from a different perspective." His solution to this critical problem, however, was for the administrator to go to the workbench or for the worker to go to the administrator's office, to exchange viewpoints "so that both will see the process in the same light. Then they would see the process from all sides and problems would be solved—and you would see how many of the demands made on labor today would be withdrawn."[35] He implicitly reduced the problems produced by the material realities of the hierarchical division of labor and class conflict to a "failure to communicate," in the words of the sadistic prison warden explaining the reason for his physical abuse of an inmate in the 1967 movie *Cool Hand Luke*. Che recognized that "sometimes a labor union leader talks to the administrator and the rank and file considers that a sellout," but he explains that problem in social-psychological language in terms of "attitudes that have to disappear because our great task of industrializing the nation cannot be accomplished if they remain with us," misunderstanding the social-structural divisions in the factory and society.[36]

Although Guevara supported the "participation" of the workers in the administration of enterprises, he would not even consider anything resembling workers' control of production. When the French left-wing agronomist René Dumont tried to convince Guevara to encourage the kind of participation in agricultural cooperatives that "would give the members the impression that the cooperative really belonged to them, *a sense of co-ownership*, and a personal attachment to the collective," Che, according to Dumont, reacted violently and argued back that "it is not a sense of ownership that they should be given, but rather a *sense of responsibility*."[37] Guevara was arguing for workers to have responsibility, but without power. That became quite explicit with the workers' groups that he created during his tenure as minister of industry in the early 1960s to deal with the various problems that the regime was facing in the economy. Among these groups were the technical advisory councils and the grievance commissions. In 1960, the government established technical advisory councils in nationalized enterprises, allegedly to encourage worker participation in management. However, these councils pursued, at best, only educational goals, since they were never given any collective decision-making power. Che Guevara stressed their educational character when he proclaimed in a speech to a national convention of technical advisory councils that his hope was that the councils would make the workers understand that they had to "sacrifice an easy demand today to achieve a greater and more solid progress in the future."[38] In fact, Guevara, with the rest of the revolutionary leaders, made the decision-making power in the nationalized industries the exclusive prerogative of the management appointed by the central government, which he so aptly described as "collective discussions, one-man decision-making and responsibility."[39] When the councils were abolished in 1962, Guevara explained that they had been only a first effort to "establish meaningful links between workers and plant management. At that time, we manifested great prejudices about the ability of the working class to elect their membership adequately. . . . Mass participation in the elections was poor. The elections were bureaucratic."[40]

Shortly after the technical advisory councils were created, the tremendous power that the state had acquired over the whole economy confronted it with the far-from-simple need to design mechanisms to address the inevitable workers' complaints in every workplace. Initially, these complaints were handled at the lowest workplace level by grievance commissions (*comisiones de reclamaciones*) that existed from 1961 until 1964. The workers, local management, and the Ministry of Labor jointly elected these commissions, although the ministry maintained the exclusive right to issue any final decision on any labor dispute.[41] It seems, however, that some grievance commissions turned out to be too lenient from the government's point of view, as they often took the side of the workers against management. This led Guevara, then minister of industry, to complain that "the grievance commissions are a barrier creating contradictions. . . . [They] will be able to accomplish a very useful task only provided that they change their attitude. Production is the fundamental task."[42]

Che Guevara, Civil Liberties, and Revolution

If we think about a socialist democracy as a society in which the vast majority of people control the principal sources of economic, social, and political power, and as an authentic participatory democracy based on the self-mobilization of the people, there is no doubt that majority rule would need to be complemented by ample minority rights and civil liberties. There can be no real socialist democracy, or for that matter full and genuine innovation and progress, with dissident individuals and minorities terrorized into silence and conformity and forcefully prevented from becoming new majorities.

By 1961, when the Cuban government, of which Che Guevara was a leading figure, finally took the step of officially declaring itself to be "socialist," it had achieved an almost total control of the polity, economy, and society along the lines of the ruling classes in the Soviet Union, China, and Eastern Europe. Cuba was well on the way to becoming a one-party state, with the government increasingly controlling all social, political, and economic life in the country. This process inevitably involved the elimination of civil liberties for individuals and groups on the island. This became evident in numerous ways ranging from the monolithic mass media totally controlled by the state to the government's later organization of incidents of mob violence (*actos de repudio*) to intimidate peaceful opponents.

As early as 1954, when observing the Guatemalan reform process that would start him on the road to becoming an independent Communist, Guevara noted the role Guatemalan newspapers played in creating a political atmosphere hostile to President Árbenz's program. He wrote to his aunt Beatriz, "If I were Árbenz, I'd close them down in five minutes."[43] He got his wish six years later, not in Guatemala but in Cuba. In May 1960, Che was among the key leaders of the revolutionary government who presided over the suppression of the opposition and independent press, accelerating the creation of a politically monolithic mass media system that continues to exist until today. To be sure, the "free press" that existed in Cuba before the revolution was hardly a paragon of democracy. The media was officially censored for much of the time that Batista was in power (1952–58) but it was quite open before then, except for the recurrent Cold War government encroachments on the significant Communist media. Of course, even then, freedom of the press was for the most part restricted to the very wealthy individuals and corporations that had the capital to own and operate major mass media organs. But the mass media system that Che Guevara helped to establish in the mid-1960s was totally monolithic and thus far less democratic than what had ever preceded it in Cuba.

Contrary to beliefs that have long been held by many liberals and leftists in the United States and elsewhere, the elimination of freedom of the press and other civil liberties was not merely a reaction to the powerful hostile pressures of US imperialism, much less internal class forces in Cuba. For one thing, there was no major external or internal threat to the stability of the revolutionary government when the mass media was seized in mid-1960. Undoubtedly, the revolutionary leaders acted under serious internal and external constraints. The strong opposition of the US empire to anything that would disturb the economic, political, and foreign policy status quo in its "backyard" weighed heavily on the political calculus of the revolutionary leaders. But at least as important was that these leaders had a political and ideological view of reality that shaped their perceptions of danger, their appropriate responses to it, and especially what they regarded as the desirable form of social and political organization, with the Soviet model being an increasingly important reference point.

At the time that freedom of the press was eliminated in Cuba, not only did Guevara see himself as a Marxist, but he was also quite familiar with the Marxist classics. Yet, his reading and understanding of the classical Marxist tradition seem to have been quite selective. He ignored that Marx and Engels took for granted that there would be many different views under socialism, which would be the culmination of the battle of the working class for democracy. Indeed, the Paris Commune, which was celebrated by the two socialist pioneers, included a wide range of political views and publications among its supporters and defenders. At that time, Guevara looked to the Soviet Union as a model of socialism, but he curiously ignored Lenin's views right before the October Revolution about how the press should be organized in Soviet Russia. In September 1917, shortly before coming to power, Lenin, basing himself on the political assumptions of classical Marxism, proposed:

> State power in the shape of the Soviets takes *all* the printing presses and *all* the newsprint and distributes them *equitably*: the state should come first—in the interests of the majority of the people, the majority

of the poor, particularly the majority of the peasants, who for centuries have been tormented, crushed and stultified by the landowners and the capitalists.

The big parties should come second—say, those that have polled one or two hundred thousand votes in both capitals. The smaller parties should come third, and then any group of citizens, which has a certain number of members or has collected a certain number of signatures.[44]

In early November, shortly after the triumph of the revolution, Lenin suggested ten thousand as the number of citizens forming a group entitled to press facilities.[45]

During the days in the Sierra Maestra, while Guevara demonstrated his courage, intelligence, and leadership skills to rise to the top level of the guerrilla army, he also saw himself as a hard-liner, or, as he himself put it, one of the "more drastic ones."[46] This was consistent with his independent but very hard Communist views regarding "bourgeois freedoms" that were far from the "humanist" philosophy that some sympathizers have attributed to him. During his days in the Sierra, Guevara opposed Fidel Castro's very effective tactic of returning prisoners (minus their weapons) to the enemy, a tactic that made a great deal of sense when facing a mercenary and demoralized army with no social or political support among the population at large.[47] In consonance with being one of the "more drastic ones," Guevara volunteered to execute the infamous traitor Eutímio Guerra. As Guevara described it in his private diary, "the situation was uncomfortable for the people and for [Eutímio] so I ended the problem giving him a shot with a .32 [caliber] pistol in the right side of the brain, with exit orifice in the right temporal [lobe]. He gasped a little while and was dead."[48] Che Guevara's "hard line" policies also had strong ascetic and puritan elements, although its effects were checked and reversed before the establishment of Cuba's one-party state. Thus, when his troops occupied the town of Sancti Spiritus in central Cuba in late 1958, he tried to ban alcohol and the lottery, but gave up in the face of the townspeople's resistance.[49]

After the overthrow of Batista on January 1, 1959, Guevara was personally responsible for supervising some of the repressive activities of the revolutionary regime. He was the head of La Cabaña military fortress, where several hundred executions were carried out in the early months of

1959. The great majority of those executed were guilty of serious crimes and atrocities, but given the summary nature of the procedures, it cannot be ruled out that there were some innocent people whose executions were carried out at least in part because of Che Guevara's political views. It is also possible that some Batistianos may have suffered punishments quite disproportionate to the offense with which they were properly charged. The historian Lillian Guerra has presented evidence suggesting that Che Guevara repressed and executed some people not because they had killed anybody or committed atrocities but because of their anti-Communist activities, whether inside or outside Batista's government. This is an area that requires much additional historical investigation, particularly in the light of recurring charges by those who accuse Guevara of grave excesses and crimes at La Cabaña.[50]

More enduring in its consequences was Guevara's principal role in setting up Cuba's first civilian labor camp in the Guanahacabibes region in the westernmost part of Cuba in the early 1960s to confine people who had committed no crime punishable by law, revolutionary or otherwise. Che defended his actions with his usual frankness:

> [We] only send to Guanahacabibes those doubtful cases where we are not sure people should go to jail. I believe that people who should go to jail should go to jail anyway. Whether long-standing militants or whatever, they should go to jail. We send to Guanahacabibes those people who should not go to jail, people who have committed crimes against revolutionary morals, to a greater or lesser degree, along with simultaneous sanctions like being deprived of their posts, and in other cases not those sanctions, but rather to be reeducated through labor. It is hard labor, not brute labor, rather the working conditions are harsh, but they are not brutal.[51]

In the case of the Ministry of Industry under Che Guevara, it seems that people were sent to Guanahacabibes for undisciplined and immoral behavior, or of minor failures at work, and the ministry determined the sanction of various weeks or months—typically one, three, six, or twelve months[52]—working at the camp, with the right of appeal within the ministry. After completing the sentence at the labor camp, the sanctioned employee would return to his or her usual job.[53] However, it is important to keep in mind that among the people sanctioned to hard labor were those who had committed relatively minor work-related offenses. Thus, for example, Manuel Marzoa Malvezado, an executive in the chemical industry, was sanctioned to spend one month doing hard labor in Guah-anacabibes because he had recruited a specialist to transfer from another Ministry of Industry institution to his own without the appropriate vice ministerial approval, or in Marzoa's version of events, for contracting an engineer for a management role without authorization from the relevant vice minister.[54] Under either set of circumstances, it was a highly dis-proportionate, administrative and therefore nonjudicial punishment for what was, after all, a relatively minor work-related offense.

Guevara played a key role in inaugurating a tradition of administra-tive, nonjudicial detention subject to no written rules or laws and solely based on the discretion of top leaders and administrators. Since Min-istry employees who refused to accept the punishment lost their jobs, the sanctions could hardly be described as voluntary.[55] A few years later, when Guevara was no longer in the Cuban government, this administra-tive, nonjudicial approach was used in the UMAP (Unidades Militares de Ayuda a la Producción – Military Units to Aid Production) camps, although with much greater harshness, for the confinement of dissidents and social "deviants": homosexuals, members of the Jehovah Witness sect, Catholic activists, practitioners of secret Afro-Cuban religions such as Abakuá, and nonpolitical rebels. In the 1980s and until 1993, this non-judicial, forced confinement was also applied to people with AIDS.

The Relationship between Revolution and Civil Liberties

Unfortunately, there is a widely shared assumption that civil liberties are irrelevant in the context of a social revolution, particularly in an econom-ically less developed country. To be sure, even the most democratic of socialist revolutions led by the working class and its allies will be con-fronted with strong and forceful resistance by the defeated ruling classes. Moreover, some members of the exploited and oppressed groups that have been politically and ideologically influenced by the old ruling classes will aid and support the resistance of their class rulers. In light of this, the new revolutionary government will need to suppress violent and subversive acts against the new socialist system in order to defend itself. Moreover, the revolutionary government cannot wait until these violent acts take place, but must try to prevent their occurrence whenever possible. In order to do this successfully, the government will also be forced, in specific instances, to curtail the civil liberties of those actively supporting the violent opponents of the revolution—for example, to detain individuals who are providing or helping to provide supplies to a counterrevolutionary force.

But this does not justify all actions that a revolutionary government may take. The experiences of the Cuban and many social revolutions that have taken place since the early part of the twentieth century force us to confront the issue of how to preserve their original democratic character, particularly since we now know that revolutions can be defeated from the inside as well as from the outside. If socialism means the rule of the working class and its popular allies, it cannot be realized unless it is accompanied by the fullest degree of democracy. The capitalist class has been able through its private ownership and control of the economy to survive and thrive under the most diverse political systems ranging from liberal democracy to South African apartheid, Italian Fascism, and German Nazism. But because the working class and its popular allies will not privately own the economy under socialism, they can only rule society through their democratic political control of the economy and polity.

While there may undoubtedly be objective factors (imperialist intervention, severe economic crisis, and warfare, to name the most serious) that may doom a revolution or help to subvert its democratic character, there is also a powerful ideological and political legacy that has made a virtue out of the necessity of the immediate postrevolutionary period and proclaims that revolution and democracy are necessarily incompatible. It is in response to this ideological legacy that it is critical to insist that the repression that the revolutionary government will be forced to carry out, particularly right after the overthrow of the old ruling classes, can be justified and controlled by democratic aims and purposes. With the benefit of the hindsight provided by the experiences of the social revolutions that have taken place since the early part of the twentieth century, we can develop a method to address the problem of revolution and democracy, even though of course "hard cases" cannot be solved in advance, nor can every eventuality be anticipated. Daniel Bensaïd, one of the leaders of the May 1968 revolt in France, argued that while of course no rule can respond in advance to all concrete situations, "at least it makes it possible to designate and circumscribe the exception, instead of banalising it."[56]

First of all, repression can be limited and controlled in its effects if it is guided by the general criteria that repressive acts be proportional, relevant, and specific to the scope and nature of the counterrevolutionary acts committed and should last only as long as the threat that brought it about persists.[57] Moreover, punishment should generally be applied selectively to the actual individuals and specific groups involved in pre-paring and/or committing those acts, and not against broad categories of people. In other words, collective punishments should be avoided.[58] While organized revolutionary violence will be essential to the survival and safeguarding of a new revolutionary society, this is not the same as indiscriminate state terror that strikes down the guilty as well as the innocent, not because they are unintended casualties, or because of the pressure of unanticipated situations and events, but by design.[59] This is part of what Daniel Bensaïd called the development of a culture of dom-inated [or controlled] violence, which he suggests could be built on the few pointers already sketched by certain military codes and martial arts.[60]

Guevara's *Socialism and Man in Cuba*[61]

Having discussed Guevara's views and actions regarding revolutionary strategy and the road to power in chapter 2 and such varied issues as strikes, workers' representation, and civil liberties in this chapter, it would be useful to turn to a broader consideration of his overall political ideas and philosophy at the time he had become one of the most important leaders of the Cuban Revolution. More than any other revolutionary leader on the island, Guevara clearly laid out his general theory and views in *Socialism and Man in Cuba*, which he considered his most finished work.[62] In it, Che molded and shaped his vision of the New Man to be forged by Cuban Communism: a selfless and idealistic man, infused with the values and practices of heroism, dedicated to the good of society.[63]

Socialism and Man in Cuba's focus was on the individual's sacrifice for the collective good. Little if any room was left for individual self-ful-fillment, expression, and freedom and their close relationship with the collective good that Marx had thoroughly explored, especially in his early writings. When Guevara does write in *Socialism and Man in Cuba* about the individual's "greater fulfillment" and "greater inner wealth," it is in the context of taking on many more social responsibilities and sacrificing for society.[64] For Guevara's "new man," work is a social duty that—together with the development of technology on one hand, and voluntary labor, on the other hand—would achieve "his full human condition when he produces without being compelled by the physical necessity of selling himself as a commodity."[65] The problem of course was that while Guevara did not and probably could not do very much to bring about the development of technology in the island, he increasingly had to rely on voluntary labor and moral incentives to rid the country "of the erroneous view—appropriate only to a society based on exploitation—that work is a disagreeable human necessity,"[66] thereby increasing, although with good intentions, the exploitation of Cuba's workers and peasants. Moreover, Guevara's ascetic attitude toward consumer goods aimed to suppress rather than satisfy the material needs of the Cuban people. In light of this and his faith in the Communist one-party state, it was the establishment of economic equality and opposition to competition and the market, rather than the overcoming of capitalist class rule through the self-emancipation of the exploited and oppressed, that remained as the true essence of his vision of socialism and Communism.

Guevara's *Socialism and Man in Cuba* and the Transition to Communism

In *Socialism and Man in Cuba*, Guevara argues that socialism cannot be built with the worn-out weapons of capitalism and that the new man must "construct communism simultaneously with the material base of our society."[67] According to Guevara, the instruments to be used to mobilize the masses to achieve these ends must be of a fundamentally moral nature, although material incentives, especially those of a social nature, can also be used.[68] Guevara did not clarify whether he was simply criticizing, by implication, the economic practices resulting in increasing inequality in the Soviet Union or whether his critique extended to the views of Marx himself as formulated in the *Critique of the Gotha Program* and other writings. Instead, he obfuscated Marx's views on the transition from capitalism to socialism. Thus, in *Socialism and Man in Cuba*, Guevara stated that "we are not before a pure transition period such as that envisioned by Marx in the *Critique of the Gotha Program*" and indicated that we are instead facing "a new phase not foreseen by him—the first period in the transition to communism or in the construction of socialism."[69] It is impossible to tell what Che Guevara had in mind when he wrote these lines, but they certainly failed to convey anything that substantially differed from Marx's view about the transition to the higher form of communism.[70] At the time, this might have been Che's way of avoiding a frontal confrontation with Marx's political economy precisely because Guevara was actually putting forward, in overall terms, a far more voluntarist theory and perspective (the simultaneous construction of communism and socialism) than that of the German socialist pioneer.

Had Guevara accepted Marx's notion that the principle of "from each according to his ability and to each according to his work" was the one appropriate to "socialism" or the "lower stage of communism," he could have still made a meaningful contribution to historical materialism and argued that the "higher stage" of Communism cannot mechanically come about only after the "lower stage" of socialism has been completed, but that under socialism changes can be introduced that point in the direction and prepare the ground for Communism. However, Guevara goes much further in a voluntaristic direction, suggesting that "morality" and "consciousness" can somehow make up for material scarcity. While he wrote about the need to develop technology, there was a deafening silence in *Socialism and Man in Cuba* about substantially increasing consumer goods and, more generally, about raising the standard of living of the Cuban population. After all, this was a key element of the great deal of popular support enjoyed by the Cuban revolutionary government at the time. As indicated in chapter 1, for the ascetic Guevara, as it had been for the ascetic Gandhi, the idol of Che's youth, consumer goods were at best unimportant.

We must also pose the question of what Guevara's call for heroism, sacrifice, and moral incentives meant in the context of a one-party state with a domesticated official trade union organization and without political democracy, institutions of workers' control, or the right to strike. Guevara's "voluntary labor," which might have elicited an enthusiastic participation in the early years of the revolution and temporarily helped to resolve labor shortages, was bound to become a ritualistic exercise encroaching on the workers' rest and leisure time with diminishing economic returns. Voluntary labor could also involve vast economic waste, as in the case of urban workers and students going to work in the countryside, which resulted in the expenditure of more resources transporting, housing, and feeding the volunteers than any increase in agricultural output, let alone the possible waste and damage to agricultural tools, inputs, and machinery by the large-scale use of people without training and experience in agricultural tasks.

The Politics of *Socialism and Man in Cuba*

It was only in the 1970s, several years after the murder of Che Guevara in Bolivia, that the Cuban government "institutionalized" the revolution by establishing a formal political system that pretended to be democratic.[71] Before then, Che and all the other revolutionary leaders claimed that an informal, substantive, and direct democracy had been established in the country. *Socialism and Man in Cuba* clearly shows Che Guevara's strong admiration for Fidel Castro's personalistic "caudillo" methods of political rule, although Guevara vaguely concedes the need for "a more structured relationship with the masses" that must improve "in years to come."[72] Nevertheless, Che held on to Fidel Castro's supposedly intuitive method of listening to the general reactions of the people. He described how at the great mass meetings, one could observe "something like the dialogue of two tuning forks whose vibrations summon forth new vibrations each in the other. Fidel and the masses begin to vibrate in a dialogue of increasing intensity until it reaches an abrupt climax crowned by cries of struggle and of victory." Perhaps realizing that this sounded more like D. H. Lawrence's description of a sexual orgasm than the way that socialist democracy was supposedly accomplished in Cuba, Guevara quickly shifts to a supposedly Marxist-Hegelian language to justify the methods used by the revolutionary leadership. For anyone who has not lived the revolutionary experience, he argues, it is difficult to understand "the close dialectical unity that exists between the individual and the mass, in which both are interrelated, and the mass, as a whole composed of individuals, is in turn interrelated with the leader."[73]

Fidel Castro famously used gigantic rallies in moments of political crisis to mobilize support for his new major policies, rallies that did not allow for any discussion or any kind of expression of demands by autonomous popular groups. They were used only to rubber-stamp the major decisions that Castro and his close inner circle had already made. There is no doubt that, especially in the early years of the revolution, the crowds were enthusiastic and their support for the government and its policies was genuine. But these rallies were not even popular plebiscites and were far from showing any type of genuine interaction between mass and leader, for which the use of the term "dialectical" was far more apologia than Marxist philosophy.[74] Like Castro, Che utilized the dialectic not as an authentic Marxist concept or analytical tool but to justify whatever policies the government wanted to pursue.[75]

The Problem of Democratic Representation

Elsewhere in *Socialism and Man in Cuba*, Guevara states that "our greatest restraint has been the fear that any formal aspect [of political representation] might separate us from the masses and the individual, making us lose sight of the ultimate and most important revolutionary ambition: to see man liberated from his alienation."[76] Thus, formality for Guevara signifies the leadership's "separation from the masses" and is an obstacle to the elimination of alienation. Besides approving the pseudo plebiscitarian ritual of the masses' approval of the pre-ordained policies of the leadership, Che expressed no interest in designing any concrete means to structure autonomous participation and decision-making from the bottom up, whether directly at the workplace and in the community or indirectly through the free election of representatives, with the right of recall, which would allow the masses to make decisions at the national level over the polity, economy, and society as a whole. Seen in this light, it is the structurelessness of informality that leads to an increase of popular alienation from social and political power, not formality, as Che claimed.[77]

Although Guevara's *Socialism and Man in Cuba* argues that the vanguard party must become a mass party, this can only happen "when the masses have attained the level of development of the vanguard, that is, when they are educated for communism."[78] How do we know when they have been educated for communism? Guevara doesn't explicitly answer the question, but abandoning any dialectical pretense, he proclaims that "our work is aimed at providing that [communist] education."[79] Yet, a central tenet of Marx's worldview and socialism is the notion, as he argued in the *Theses on Feuerbach*, that the educator needs to be educated.

Guevara also argues, in an explicit politically elitist fashion, that because the masses are insufficiently acquainted with the new values and perceive reality only partially, they must be subjected to incentives and pressures by vanguard groups that are more ideologically advanced. That is why Guevara arrives at the Stalinist conclusion that the dictatorship of the proletariat operates "not only over the defeated class but also individually over the victorious class," through a "conscious" vanguard elite that will decide in some undefined fashion if and when the people are educated enough to participate in deciding their collective and individual fate.[80]

The Absence of Politics

Socialism and Man in Cuba is silent on one of the critical questions that any socialist social system, particularly in an economically less developed country, will inevitably face: how to set priorities. This in turn requires political discussion and debate to determine the relative importance of various and perhaps conflicting goals. Thus, what is truly remarkable about *Socialism and Man in Cuba* is that while it is very concerned about ending alienation through the elimination of competition and the market, it says absolutely nothing about the single most important way to eliminate alienation: working people controlling their fate by making democratic decisions about social, economic, and political matters. In fact, it has no working-class or popular politics at all. The clear implication is that whatever politics exist are the exclusive domain of the vanguard party and the leadership, which apparently always know best. While the pamphlet is vocal in its opposition to the capitalist market and competitive system that tends to commodify everything, including human relations, and in its praise for the individual's selfless dedication to the collectivity, opposition to the capitalist market and to the commodity form can in fact be the basis for a reactionary utopianism attempting to emulate pre-capitalist social formations. It certainly does not equal socialism, if we mean a society in which the working class and its class allies take control over their fate via a thorough democratizing of the economy, polity, and society as a whole.

Misunderstanding Guevara's Concept of Love

Some leftists have praised but misunderstood other pronouncements that Guevara makes in *Socialism and Man in Cuba*, such as his often quoted statement: "Let me say, with the risk of appearing ridiculous, that the true revolutionary is guided by strong feelings of love. It is impossible to think of an authentic revolutionary without this quality." This is a marvelous sentiment and is often cited to portray Guevara as a warm, affectionate, and loving revolutionary. The problem with this interpretation is that a few lines further down in the same paragraph, Guevara explains, while "our vanguard revolutionaries must idealize their love for the people," "they cannot descend, with small doses of daily affection, to the places where ordinary men put their love in practice."[81] In other words, this is not love as most people understand it, but rather an abstract love of the people by those at the pinnacle of the political hierarchy, without a concrete human object. In fact, Guevara's approach plays into the hoary conservative critique of revolutionaries that they love humanity but hate actual people. In this instance, Guevara's approach to love is another example of his tendency to hypostatize society at the expense of the individual and seems to have been reinforced by aspects of his personality, as when he lamented "certain character traits which make it difficult for me to get close to people."[82] In any case, two years later Guevara was saying something very different in his "Message to the Tricontinental" sent from Bolivia in April 1967. In that message he proclaimed "hatred as an element of struggle, relentless hatred of the enemy that transforms us into effective, violent, selective, and cold killing machines. Our soldiers must be thus; a people without hatred cannot vanquish a brutal enemy."[83]

Che Guevara and the Communist Model

Paco Ignacio Taibo II has written that it is curious that Che, who had been so critical of the economic policies followed by the Soviet Union, did not have a minimal awareness of the social disaster, the political authoritarianism, and repressive character of Soviet society. Taibo concludes that Guevara was a prisoner of what he labeled "Neanderthal Marxism."[84]

Since his experience in Guatemala, when he became radicalized, Ernesto Guevara adopted and remained committed to the Soviet Union's Communist system model in its fundamental structural outlines, even though not necessarily with regard to certain specific economic and cultural policies such as socialist realism in the arts. The key structural features of Communism as a social system included the establishment of a one-party state in control of the social, political, and economic life of the society through the so-called mass organizations, such as the official trade unions and women's organizations, acting as transmission belts for the single ruling party. The efforts of the single party and the mass organizations to control the population have been supplemented by the political police as the principal organ of repression, which has historically been directed not only against foreign interference (such as the US intelligence services plotting against the Cuban government) but also against domestic dissidents and opponents, regardless of how home-grown and legitimate their grievances might be. This system was consolidated under Joseph Stalin in the Soviet Union, and after World War II, the invading Soviet Army extended its reach to Eastern Europe. Revolutions in other parts of the world established versions of the same system in countries such as China, Vietnam, and Cuba. There were differences among the systems established in these countries, as well as between them and the Soviet Union. But the same has been true for capitalism in countries such as Japan, the United States, and Sweden, which remain capitalist since they all maintain the essential elements of the capitalist system in terms of the primacy of the private corporate sector, capital accumulation and exploitation, the profit system, and other key elements of the system.

This top-down political vision also explains why Guevara never saw popular election of representatives as central to the process of the emancipation of the exploited and oppressed. Properly understood, the popular election of representatives is not merely an instrumental, pragmatic tool, but a process of decision-making that is inextricably connected to political discussion, education, and self-government. Earlier revolutionary movements, such as the Paris Commune and the soviets of the 1905 and 1917 revolutions, placed a major emphasis on the deliberative and legislative, as well as the executive, powers of the people at the base. However, Guevara explicitly rejected the notion that democratic discussion and decision-making could be applied to the noncombat aspects of military life in his 1960 treatise on guerrilla warfare, which was perhaps his most open-ended and least dogmatic work. Moreover, he also glossed over the importance of the election of representatives among the people ruled by the guerrilla armies when he proposed that "in view of the importance of relations with the peasants, it is necessary to create organizations that make regulations for them, organizations that exist not only within the liberated area, but also have connections in the adjacent areas."[85] Che spelled out no democratic representative mechanisms through which the peasants could learn through practice to rule themselves. In the guerrilla scenarios discussed by Guevara, the potential influence of the mass media or competing political parties were of little importance.

Closely connected to Guevara's avoidance and rejection of the popular election of representatives was the virtually obsessive fear that he shared with Fidel and Raúl Castro about divisions among the revolutionary leaders and the people at large. They saw any kind of genuine elections as creating divisions that they had to suppress for the sake of unity. Their fear was reinforced by the negative effects of divisions among the revolutionary leaders that they witnessed in countries such as Algeria, which ended with the overthrow of Ahmed Ben Bella, a close friend and ally of the Cuban leaders. Whatever significant political differences may have existed among the revolutionary rulers have never been revealed to the public, except when people have been purged from the leadership and, of course, with the public only hearing the side of those who won the fight and remained in power.[86] This is the "monolithic unity" that Raúl Castro, along with the other revolutionary leaders, has invoked through close to six decades in power.[87]

The supposed unity of the Cuban people advocated early on by Che Guevara, Raúl Castro, and the PSP has been used to justify the monopoly on power that the Cuban Communist Party holds. In fact, the Cuban people have never been "united" in the sense of having transcended class, race, and many other kinds of politically and socially rooted conflicts. And the Cuban working class, much less the Cuban nation (in the name of which the CCP rules), is by no means homogeneous. As Leon Trotsky argued against the similar Stalinist notion of homogeneity and unity:

> In reality, classes are heterogeneous; they are torn by inner antagonisms, and arrive at the solution of common problems not otherwise than through an inner struggle of tendencies, groups, and parties. It is possible, with certain qualifications, to concede that "a party is part of a class." But since a class has many "parts"—some look forward and some look back—one and the same class may create several parties. For the same reason one party may rest upon parts of different classes. An example of only one party corresponding to one class is not to be found on the whole course of political history—provided, of course, you do not take the police appearance for the reality.[88]

Besides having supported to the end of his life the one-party state as an essential element of the Communist system he believed in, Guevara also upheld, during the years he held power and helped to shape the destiny of the Cuban Revolution, "democratic centralism," the key mechanism used by the Communist parties built on the Stalinist model to maintain unanimity and suppress internal dissent. As he told Maurice Zeitlin in 1961, the democratic centralism practiced in the Soviet Union meant that "regional organizations have the authority to discuss measures, and their decisions are communicated through ascending organizations to the top," a Soviet textbook description that had little connection to the reality of the power exercised by the Political Bureau and Central Committee of the Communist Party of the Soviet Union.[89] When pressed by Zeitlin about the fact that factions were not going to be allowed in the new ruling party in Cuba and that this might lead to the quashing of dissent by those in power, Guevara responded by distinguishing factionalism from dissent and cited the wide differences that were expressed inside cabinet meetings. Yet whatever "dissent" may have been expressed inside cabinet meetings was usually not revealed to the Cuban people. Guevara went on to condemn cases when "after free discussion and a majority decision, a defeated minority works outside of, and against, the party—as Trotsky did, for example. To do so is counterrevolutionary."[90] However, it must be noted that in the mid-sixties, after Guevara had resigned from the Cuban government and given up his Cuban citizenship to engage in guerrilla warfare abroad, he privately wondered whether the term "democratic centralism" had retained any specific meaning, noting that it was a widely disseminated myth hiding the most diverse political structures and thus lacking, for him, any real content.[91] Nevertheless, he expressed no judgment or criticism about the particular way in which "democratic centralism" was being applied in the Cuban Communist Party and in the so-called mass organizations (such as the unions and women's federation).

Conclusion: The Problem of Socialism and Democracy

The predominant revolutionary currents in Latin America during most of the first half of the twentieth century tended to see democracy as an irrelevant bourgeois notion. In light of the degree of poverty, lack of economic development, and subjection to imperialism prevalent in the continent, socialism was about feeding the masses, establishing economic equality, and freeing the country from imperialism. This required a powerful revolutionary state, a Hobbesian machine, to bring about these highly desirable goals. How this state would be controlled from below was not an issue. Rather, this current of thought emphasized how those in power were honest, intransigent, and convinced revolutionaries. Far more often than not, the notion of people empowering themselves to make decisions and take control of their fate was not even considered except by distinct minority currents within the revolutionary movement.

Guevara's politics was a variant of this kind of Latin American leftism, which was particularly influential during his young adult years—in the late 1940s and early 1950s—coinciding with the early phases of the Cold War. It was especially during that period that the US State Department was supporting a large number of corrupt and brutal Latin American dictatorships as supposed bulwarks against Communism. The US intervention in Guatemala, of which Guevara was a personal witness, confirmed to millions of Latin Americans that the United States was no friend of reform, much less of revolution, and had absolutely no respect for national self-determination and sovereignty. While Latin American social democracy gave lip service to structural social reform, it joined the American camp in the Cold War and abandoned whatever degree of anti-imperialism it might have displayed in the past. In the Latin American countries where governments had been elected in at least relatively free elections, unprincipled politicking among the established political parties leading to public corruption were serious problems and little, if anything, had been done to reduce the vastly unequal distribution of land, wealth, and income. The Latin American media, even when not censored by dictatorships, was under the control of big capitalist interests and depended on the heavily biased North American news services such as the Associated Press and the United Press for content.

In the face of such realities, Communism seemed a real alternative to many young Latin Americans sincerely concerned about the fate of the poor and oppressed. Implicit in this ideological and political choice was a politics from above, at least in the sense that the people in general could not be trusted to make their own choices. In this worldview, which Che embraced, people could be easily diverted from the socialist goal by any number of forces, including the capitalist and imperialist propaganda of the mass media, as well as the expectation of immediate improvements in their standard of living. They could not be trusted to make the sacrifices necessary to build the new society unless they were compelled to through a combination of the exhortation and personal example set by the revolutionary leaders, wholesale censorship, and the suppression of competing political parties. The generalized scarcity of consumer goods produced by the economic retaliation of US imperialism, domestic economic inefficiency and waste, and the government planners' bias against those types of goods made such sacrifices compulsory for the great majority of the population.

Building an Alternative

As the legacy of the traditional social democratic and Communist parties becomes increasingly diluted and loses influence over the new political generations, other organizational experiments and political currents have developed in Latin America, Europe, and Africa. They may draw on past revolutionary ideas and political movements that have aimed at democratizing all of society, to transcend the relationship between liberal democracy and an economic system that depends on maintaining exploitation and inequality, thereby distorting and infringing on the democratic character of the political system itself. These movements involved attempts to design various means to empower the rank and file to participate in policy-making, thus turning over to them the responsibility of power. One such participatory means was designed by the Paris Commune of 1871, which established the immediate right of recall of elected representatives who were compensated with average salaries in the general context of an economically egalitarian society. Similar attempts were made by the Russian Soviets (or workers' councils) in the revolutions of 1905 and October 1917, although in the latter case the Soviets lost their multiparty democratic character during the Civil War (1918–20), leading first to the dictatorial methods of "Leninism in power" and later to Stalin's totalitarian system.[92] Subsequent revolutionary movements were influenced by this tradition: the German Revolution of 1918; the POUM (Unified Marxist Workers' Party), an anarchist alliance depicted by George Orwell in *Homage to Catalonia*; the Hungarian Workers' Council in 1956; and important tendencies in the struggles in Chile from 1970 to 1973, Portugal (after the death of the dictator Salazar) from 1974 to 1975, Iran in 1979, and Poland in 1980–81.[93] Unfortunately, outside forces defeated and cut short the time necessary to consolidate and improve many of these vital revolutionary experiments.

Chapter Four

Che Guevara's Political Economy

Che Guevara and the Cuban Economy

Before the victory of the Cuban Revolution on January 1, 1959, Che Guevara only had the administrative and economic experience of ruling over "liberated areas" in the Sierra Maestra, where he established artisan workshops to make his troops as self-supporting as possible. Later on, the control he gained over parts of Las Villas province in central Cuba only lasted for a very short period before Batista fled the country at the end of 1958.

As we saw in chapter 3, right after he arrived in Havana, in the first days of 1959, Che was put in charge of La Cabaña fortress, one of the most important military installations in the country. After a long period of travel through Asia and Africa that summer, he was appointed to head the National Bank of Cuba (roughly equivalent to the Federal Reserve in the United States) in the fall of 1959. Shortly afterward, in 1960, he became head of the industrial department of the National Institute of Agrarian Reform (Instituto Nacional de Reforma Agraria, INRA), which he continued to head when it was later separated from INRA and transformed into the Ministry of Industry (MININD) in February 1961.

We do not know the degree to which Guevara's interest in political economy led to his appointment to important economic positions in the Cuban government and how his government experience in turn increased his interest in economics. There is no doubt, however, that Marxist political economy became a central interest and concern of Guevara's. In fact, as we shall see later in this chapter, Che came to see socialism itself as centralized economic planning and the rejection of competition and the law of value. Moreover, shortly after becoming minister of industry in 1961, Guevara sponsored a seminar on Karl Marx's *Capital* where he and other high-level functionaries in the ministry studied Marx's classic work.[1] Guevara became very concerned, especially in the mid sixties, with the Soviet economy and what he saw as its drift toward capitalism. Thus, the private notebooks that he wrote at the time and published many decades later focused on the Soviet economy and were titled *Apuntes críticos a la economía política* (Critical Notes on Political Economy).

Guevara's General Outlook on Marxist Political Economy

From the moment Che Guevara became an independent Communist, he adopted the orthodox politics of the Soviet Communist political tradition, which defined socialism as the nationalization of private enterprise and the establishment of the "dictatorship of the proletariat" under the leadership of a vanguard Communist Party.[2] Guevara's Marxism, like that of many other Communists and leftists in the global South, also had a Third World inflection that emphasized the subordination and exploitation of the underdeveloped countries by the more developed ones through the latter's control of the principal industries of the less economically developed economies and the unequal exchange that they imposed on their economic dependents.[3] For Guevara, as well as for non-Marxists such as the well-known Latin American economist Raúl Prebisch, and later to the at one time hegemonic dependency theory, this unequal exchange was the inevitable result of the less developed countries exporting raw materials and agricultural goods in exchange for the industrial products manufactured in the economically developed world.[4]

Che never abandoned this orthodox Soviet conception of socialism insofar as the role of the state and the "dictatorship of the proletariat" were concerned. But he began to diverge from it on other fundamental issues. One of them involved the central question of the role of the working class as the agent of revolution in Latin America, which Guevara rejected on two counts. First, he identified the peasantry, rather than the working class, as the central force for socialism in the Third World. Second, he argued that in the developed capitalist countries, in spite of having become more cohesive and organized, the working class had turned its back on proletarian internationalism and had therefore become incapable of achieving class consciousness.[5] That is why he was also critical of Lenin's support, in his *Left-Wing Communism: An Infantile Disorder*, of Communist participation in conservative unions. Che argued that "as a general tactic it is, at least, dangerous" and can only be implemented by men of Lenin's stature, because "the contact with the mud puddle of the aristocratic proletariat perverts men and parties and opportunism easily installs itself in . . . [these] unions."[6]

What began as a disagreement on several issues had become, by the mid-1960s, a full blown critique of the USSR. According to Guevara, one could find "phenomena of expansion, non-equivalent exchange, competition, exploitation up to a point and certainly the subjugation of the weak states by the strong"[7] in the Soviet Union's drift toward capitalism. In 1965, he even claimed in a famous speech in Algiers that when the "socialist countries" engaged in international trade guided by the prices established by the world market, they were "to a certain extent, accomplices to imperialist exploitation" and therefore had "the moral duty of liquidating their tacit complicity with the exploiting countries of the West."[8] Central to this capitalist drift was what Che characterized as the Soviet Union's concessions to individual, private, noncollective economic activity and to the law of value. He attributed the origins of this drift to Lenin's New Economic Policy (NEP), "one of the greatest steps backwards of the USSR," mainly through its concessions allowing the peasantry to grow crops and trade them freely.[9] It is significant that in his *Apuntes* (Notes) of the mid-1960s Guevara arrived at that conclusion without even discussing the concrete situation—widespread hunger—that forced Lenin to adopt the NEP, in contradiction to some of Guevara's own previous writings.[10] Neither did Guevara explain how the nefarious influence of NEP could have survived beyond Stalin's brutal collectivization of the peasantry and super-exploitation of the working class. By now, politics for Guevara did not seem to be a response to concrete circumstances but the exclusive result of "ideas" or principles. He explicitly disregarded the reality of the economic crisis in the Soviet Union of the 1920s with the astonishing claim that, at the time, "there was nothing economically impossible." The only issue to be considered, he wrote, is whether "something is compatible with the development of socialist consciousness. Lenin says that the difficulty lays in awakening interest, give enough room and interest will be awakened; that is the typical petty-bourgeois greed of the peasant. To form socialists on that basis, fat chance."[11] Thus, for Che, there was no difference between the overcoming of ideological and political obstacles—by fostering a new consciousness through political struggle and education—and the overcoming of the objective economic obstacles of underdevelopment and dire scarcity.

It goes without saying that Lenin's primary concern in proposing and implementing the NEP was not the immediate conversion of peasants to socialism, but the economic survival of the regime. He thought that new collectivist possibilities would develop in the Soviet Union after the economic situation was stabilized and the growth of cooperatives had introduced the principles of collective work to the Soviet peasantry. In contrast with Guevara's voluntarism, his priority was to promote—and in fact to direct—the revolutionary movement in Western Europe with the hope that a successful socialist revolution in a developed capitalist country such as Germany would in turn help the Soviet Union develop economically.

Beyond that, it is important to consider whether the NEP or a similar economic policy was justified and necessary in 1921, not only because of the severe economic crisis experienced by post–World War I and post–civil war Soviet Russia but also because of the overwhelming dominance of peasant simple commodity producers in the country. In *Socialism: Utopian and Scientific*, Friedrich Engels made the distinction between modern capitalism, in which production has become a social act but the social product is appropriated and controlled by individual capitalists, and socialism, in which both production and its appropriation have become socialized.[12] Following this distinction, it is the productive property requiring collective work that is the proper object of socialization, not individual or family production, much less petty personal property.[13] Therefore, Soviet agriculture could not have been, for the most part, ready for any substantial collectivization, except for the viciously brutal one that Stalin carried out, starting with the first Five-Year Plan in 1928.[14]

Much of Guevara's critique of the Soviet Union derived from his conception of the political economy of socialism and communism as a uniform, monolithic society without conflicting interests of any kind, based on the assumption that class conflict is the only possible kind of social antagonism.[15] Consistent with that monolithic vision, he also cast a negative eye on the Soviet *kolkhoz* (the collective farm that allowed for small private plots, in contrast to the *sovkhoz*, a totally collectivized state farm that was fully integrated into the state economic plan), arguing that even if the *kolkhoz* were totally collectivized, their most important feature—"the contradiction between the property belonging to the whole people and the property of the individual collectivity"—would remain unchanged, an unacceptable situation from his point of view.[16] This also explains much of his critique of Lenin's NEP, as well as the co-operatives that Lenin had advocated in 1922. "The fundamental error," argued Guevara, "is to think that the collective character of the cooperatives prevails over their private character," adding, "There is a class force behind them and their legitimacy and consolidation strengthen the [peasant] class that Lenin feared so much."[17]

It is this same monolithism that explains other aspects of Guevara's political economy beyond his critique of the Soviet Union. One was his disregard for the principle of the popular election of representatives in every facet of socialist society, as I analyzed with respect to guerrilla warfare in chapter 1. So, for example, while reflecting on key economic issues confronting a socialist society, such as whether or not to postpone economic development in order to devote resources to produce needed consumption goods, he considers no mechanism by which people could make a decision on such a critical question, implying it would be decided solely by the ruling Communist Party.[18]

The same disregard for democratic mechanisms of control also led him to espouse an uncritical view of the Soviet political system. In a discussion on the atomic bomb, Che said, absurdly, that "the Soviet atomic bomb was in the hands of the people," ignoring the potential total annihilation of peoples and intrinsic inability of nuclear weapons to distinguish between combatants, civilians, the ruling classes, and the rest of the population.[19]

Guevara was very clear about the fact that the Soviet economy was not working well. He rejected the Soviet Union's claim that it had achieved the highest standard of living in the world and noted that "events have defeated this dream."[20] He was also contemptuous of the Soviet boasts about agricultural achievements, which he regarded as a mockery after the Soviet Union's purchase of wheat from the United States,[21] adding elsewhere that the United States could boast more about its agriculture than the Soviet Union despite the fact that "they are imperialists, not socialists." Guevara was not only willing to recognize the productive achievements of US agriculture but also pointed out the success of large US corporations in partially eliminating management bureaucratism, by which he meant paperwork, and their greater ability to make quick and flexible decisions.[22] It was that lack of flexibility that, according to Guevara, made it impossible for Soviet factory directors to close a plant to renovate and update it, or to increase production, for fear that the factory's productive quota would be increased to an even higher level by central planners.[23]

Guevara argued that there had been no technical progress in the Soviet Union and the mechanisms used to replace the market had become fossilized, implying a lack of fresh and even critical thinking. It is in this context that Guevara's new critical stance toward Stalin must be understood.[24] As Guevara put it:

> It is in the supposed errors of Stalin that we can see the difference between a revolutionary and a revisionist attitude. Stalin sees the danger of commodity relations and tries to confront them, breaking up what he is opposed to. The new leadership, by contrast, gives in to the impulses of the superstructure and emphasizes commodity relations, theorizing that the complete utilization of these economic levers leads to communism. There were few times when Stalin was publicly opposed, thereby demonstrating his great historic crime, with his contempt for communist education and institution of the unlimited cult of authority.[25]

While this new critical view of Stalin was welcome in light of Guevara's earlier worship of the Soviet leader, Stalin had committed far greater "historic crimes" that Guevara never acknowledged, including the creation of a ruthless totalitarian regime, mass murders, and subordination of the world Communist movement to the interests of the Soviet Union.[26] This may help to explain why, in spite of his critique of the actually existing Soviet Union, he never questioned its fundamental socialist character, however far the Soviet Union deviated from his conception of genuine socialism. In a section of his *Apuntes*, Guevara tried to answer the question of why the prediction of the *Communist Manifesto* that the elimination of class antagonism within nations would lead to the elimination of hostility among nations had not come to pass in the Soviet bloc. Guevara concluded that either a) the propositions put forward by the *Manifesto* were false, b) that they would come to pass under full Communism, perhaps in a world scale, or c) that class antagonism had not yet disappeared in the Communist bloc.[27] Guevara did not consider a fourth option: that independently of whether or not the *Manifesto*'s predictions were valid, the Soviet Union and the Eastern bloc countries were not socialist (at least according to the definition of the *Manifesto*, which took for granted the existence of a democratic political and social order) and represented instead another form of class society, albeit one not organized on the basis of private capitalist property.

Che Guevara and the "Great Debate" about the Cuban Economy

As the politics of the Cuban government shifted in a clearly Communist direction, the activities of the agricultural sector controlled by INRA were supposedly organized on the basis of the enterprise self-financing methods being implemented in the Soviet Union, which stressed material incentives.[28] In contrast, Guevara, with his growing distrust and criticism of the Soviet Union's economic system, opted to run the enterprises of the industrial (nonsugar) sector under his control on a centralized budgetary system of finance, which, as we shall explain below, emphasized moral incentives.

These two different approaches clashed in the so-called great debate that took place in Cuba from 1963 to 1965, which focused on three principal topics: the role of material and moral incentives in the construction of socialism, the proper organization of industrial enterprises in relation to the economy as a whole, and the applicability of "law of value."[29] At least by implication, the debate on these topics also involved the broader issue of whether the Soviet Union was the appropriate economic model for Cuba.[30] Guevara thought that this debate was extremely important and spent much of his time writing many articles on questions that were of the utmost importance to his view of Marxism and socialism. Yet, the debate took place almost entirely in the specialized journal *Nuestra*

Industria: Revista Económica, which was published by Guevara's Ministry of Industry, and in *Cuba Socialista*, the leading theoretical journal of
the Cuban Communist Party, which was being formed at the time and
finally established in 1965. It was therefore limited to the upper echelons
of the government and the political class, and since it was not published
or transmitted in the mass media, average Cubans were not aware of, let
alone able to participate in, this debate.

Che Guevara and Material and Moral Incentives

In the "great debate" Guevara articulated in the most "finished" fashion
his arguments in favor of moral incentives, a policy that he had already
begun to implement as head of the industrial department of INRA and
the Ministry of Industry. Moral incentives usually took the form of special citations and honors prominently displayed at the workplace, which
were sometimes published in the mass media and even in ceremonies
at which Cuba's revolutionary leaders were present. This was in consonance with Che's one-sided emphasis on "consciousness," the individual's exclusive devotion to society and duty to serve the collectivity, and
his own personal asceticism. While generally "reluctant to use material
incentives as a fundamental element," he supported some material rewards, especially those benefiting the group rather than the individual
worker, and allowed, for example, limited rewards for the overfulfill-
ment of quotas.[31] On various occasions, he suggested that good workers
should be materially rewarded with the training necessary for promotion. But his focus remained on moral incentives.

Che Guevara's views in favor of moral incentives were not limited
to Cuba. Even as he was becoming increasingly critical of the Soviet
Union, he praised the Communist work brigades in that country as
an authentic socialist movement.[32] Moreover, he pointed out at the bimonthly meeting of the top administrators of the Ministry of Industry
on October 12, 1963, that one of the causes of the Soviet Union's "agricultural catastrophe" was "the little attention given to the development
of moral stimuli."[33]

When in the first half of the 1960s, the Cuban government instituted voluntary labor as a way to deal with a variety of problems in
the economy, including serious labor shortages, it introduced a system

of competition among groups of workers ("socialist emulation") to increase production. As incentives to compete, the government resorted to a mix of material and moral rewards. By late 1965, however, material rewards had been phased out. The government established a bureaucratic apparatus to promote and administer socialist emulation and the Cuban equivalent of Stakhanovism (a system introduced by Stalin in the Soviet Union in the 1930s to have workers compete with each other in order to sharply increase production). Reinaldo Castro—no relation to the Cuban leaders—became a well-known figure in a nationwide emulation during the 1962 sugar harvest for hand-cutting about eleven tons of sugar cane a day. He was named National Hero of Work in 1964. The Cuban government even created a "millionaires movement" for the sugar workers, who, organized into brigades, had cut a million *arrobas* (1 *arroba* = 25 pounds or 11.5 kilograms). Che heaped considerable praise on both Reinaldo Castro's achievement and on the "millionaires movement."[34]

The predominance of the moral incentives policy in the Cuba of the 1960s cannot be exclusively attributed to Che Guevara's persuasiveness, prestige, and influence, however. Andrés Vilariño, a government economist of that period, indicated that the government had been pushed into adopting moral incentives as a result of the lack of equilibrium that had developed between the purchasing power of the people and the consumer goods available on the market. Purchasing power had grown without a corresponding growth in the quantity of available consumer goods, ushering in the phenomenon of "socialist inflation." As Vilariño explained, disposable income had increased during the first years of the revolution as a result of a variety of redistributive measures adopted by the government, but a variety of factors had hurt production, including errors in planning, the ignorance of the new administrators, inefficiency of state investment, and underutilization of equipment and a decrease in the labor effort.[35] Or as Fidel Castro put it years later, on November 16, 1973: "The application of material incentives is useless and ineffective in a situation of tremendous inflation. . . . When everybody has his pockets bulging with money, none of these things [wage differentials, material incentives] is effective. . . . A superabundance of money becomes a disincentive to work for many people."[36]

The debate within the government's top echelons regarding material and nonmaterial (moral) incentives assumed a basic harmony of interests between workers and managers that ignored the reality of a hierarchical division of labor in which workers had no control of the workplace, and it obscured the nature of a social order in which some ruled and others did not. In the case of moral incentives, Che's position meant that the Cuban workers had to accept responsibility for producing without any meaningful power. In the context of a one-party state, the absence of independent workers' organizations and the hegemony of a state-controlled mass media allowed the government to impose order from the top down, by a force external to the working class and the great majority of the people. Che Guevara argued that because Cuba's newly founded socialist society had not yet ceased to be a class society, it had to resort to coercive measures to impose worker discipline, complemented by education, until discipline became "spontaneous."[37] Here, as elsewhere, Guevara didn't even consider the role that working-class democratic institutional mechanisms could play in maintaining and enforcing discipline from within instead of from above. So, for example, at the bimonthly meeting of the top administrators of the Ministry of Industry on August 10, 1963, he recommended regular discussions with the enterprises run by his ministry but hastened to add that "naturally, the discussion with the [state] enterprises should take place because we must achieve the deepest knowledge of the truth, not because we have the obligation to discuss [such matters] with the enterprises. That is to say, the discussion with the enterprises is part of the operational work, in order to improve it, and is not part of representative democracy, because it does not exist at any level."[38]

Political Incentives

Because the great debate's profound ideological character obscured the real nature and distribution of power in society, the advocates of material and moral incentives did not consider a third option: political incentives. Responsibility to produce is real only when workers have the power to decide; that is, self-management at the workplace and decision-making in society at large by the whole working class and population, with a proper division between what can be decided at the local, regional, and national levels. In this model, workers have a genuine stake in what happens in the workplace and in society because everyone is working for her/himself, individually and collectively. But workers' control at the workplace entails a degree of local decision-making—and therefore of decentralization—that is contrary to Guevara's approach. Moreover, such an arrangement can only exist and thrive in a thoroughly politicized society, open to the fullest democratic debate about economic and political priorities, without the monopoly of control by a single party.

Is There a Role for Material and Moral Incentives under Socialism?

While this debate took place in the context of a society lacking even the most elementary forms of popular democratic control, it did pose questions that are also relevant to socialist democracies. In my view, the political economy of a socialist democracy with worker control of production and society would probably need to integrate, in addition to political incentives, elements of both material and nonmaterial or moral incentives, particularly in the context of an economically less developed society such as Cuba. Why would there be a need for material incentives? While Marx did not develop his theory of capitalism and the coming socialist revolution for the purposes of economic development, the unambiguous position that he took in the *Critique of the Gotha Program*—that in socialism, or the lower phase of communist society, rewards and distribution had to be calibrated according to work—is even more relevant for a less developed economy. It was only in the higher phase of communist society, with the end of the individual's subordination to the division of labor, after the productive forces have increased with the all-round development of the individual and all the springs of cooperative wealth flow more abundantly, Marx argued, that society could adopt the slogan: "From each according to his ability, to each according to his needs!"[39] Under socialism, or the lower stage of communism, the still existing material scarcity means that workers cannot obtain all the material goods they would wish to enjoy. In light of this limiting objective reality, material compensation according to work and the degree of skill involved in the work, with perhaps certain upper and lower limits and as democratically determined by state and local institutions, would be the best method of determining rewards. The use of such an approach would be clearly more objective and far less arbitrary than other criteria such as political loyalty, as has been widely practiced in Cuba, or the responsibility without power advocated by Guevara, if proper social welfare provisions are made for those unable to work and workers' control and a free trade union movement has an indispensable supervisory role over the system of rewards. Such a process would be compatible with the gradual introduction, according to the economy's real material achievements and possibilities, of free goods and services beyond free public health and education, thus anticipating and bringing closer the communist future.

Moreover, there might still remain a need for additional sources of moral inspiration from below in order to cement the political and moral cohesion of a socialist society, particularly to discipline those who resist contributing with their work to the common welfare. Here we should consider what E. P. Thompson, James C. Scott, and other social scientists have called "moral economy." The sanctions deriving from "moral economy" are bound to play an important role in any process of worker self-management to the extent that it would punish through informal social pressures any "shirking" or resistance to perform one's duties and obligations in the work process. Since working-class consciousness is very uneven, the need for these types of pressures are not going to disappear in a period of transition from capitalism to socialism and might even become more necessary under conditions granting full employment and a much greater security to workers than under capitalism. In extreme cases, this might involve social ostracism like the old British working-class custom of "sending someone to Coventry," which involved a refusal to speak to or have social contact with fellow workers who had violated elementary forms of solidarity through such actions as strike-breaking. In a sense, social ostracism could become the socialist democracy's equivalent of firing, let alone jailing, people.

It is important to note that Che Guevara did consider the issue of workers' control and self-management. As he explained in his *Apuntes* he had no problem with a worker directing an enterprise. Nor was he opposed to the possibility of workers electing a coworker, but only to perform a particular task, "not as a representative of the whole unity before the larger unity of the state, in an antagonistic form."[40] He expressed a similar viewpoint about cooperatives, which he regarded as an advance in capitalist society but a step backward under socialism, "because it places these associations in opposition to the whole society that owns the other means of production."[41]

Che argued that it was impossible to make production solely dependent on the workers collective or individual decision at the local level, but he never considered the possibility of developing democratic mechanisms to integrate local workplace with higher national levels of decision-making. Although Che conceded that rank-and-file experience and practice was crucial, particularly in the context of an inexperienced and largely ignorant central and mid-level administration, he expressed a clear preference, based on what he claimed was his experience, for a "well-situated" technical/managerial cadre, which he asserted could turn around an enterprise better than the workers themselves.[42]

Guevara also had a critical view of the Yugoslavian experience of workers' self-management, which he saw as another indication of the pitfalls of workers' control. In Yugoslavia, the system of worker self-management acquired a major economic and social weight from the 1950s until the 1970s. In reality, management made the business evaluations and decisions, but formally major decisions had to go through the blue-collar-dominated workers' councils, a process that opened the door for clientelism, corruption, passivity, and cynicism toward the principle of self-management.[43] Being a part of a system that combined "market socialism" with political authoritarianism,[44] self-management was limited to the operation of individual work centers. Political and economic power in the various regions and the country as a whole was monopolized by the one-party state embodied in Marshal Tito's League of Communists of Yugoslavia. While this locally self-managed but regionally and nationally authoritarian "market socialism" did increase worker input and decision-making and productivity at the local level, it also created unemployment, sharp trade cycles, pay inequality,[45] and especially notable regional disparities favoring the northern republics.[46] Local self-management combined with the workers' lack of political and economic power outside their workplace understandably fostered a parochial outlook among many workers and managers. As the Yugoslav scholar Mitja Kamusić pointed out, this model of self-management encouraged workers at the local level to be interested in investments that would ensure an immediate increase in their earnings, stable employment, and better working conditions, but not in investments over the long term and in other parts of the enterprise, or in the types of investment that would require reduction of manpower or its requalification. Workers were even less supportive of investments—however viable—in other enterprises, particularly those situated far away geographically.[47]

While Guevara was silent about the more positive features of the Yugoslav system, he was right in arguing that the Yugoslav model promoted the competition of factories against each other, just as under capitalism[48] and, more generally, that workers' self-management would create unfair income differentials among workers depending on the sector and factory in which they worked.[49] But more than anything, for Guevara, workers' control and self-management would foster the expression and recognition of different interests in the workplace (and beyond), which he feared could lead to an antagonistic confrontation with the state and the ruling Communist Party, the repositories, according to his still orthodox Soviet view of the nature of socialism, of genuine "class consciousness."

Che Guevara and Industrial Planning

Another important element of the "great debate" concerned the relationship between individual enterprises and the national economy as a whole. Che Guevara participated in this part of the debate as a strong proponent and defender of the "centralized budgetary system of finance" he had been implementing in the non-sugar industrial sector of the island under his Ministry of Industry. Under this system, the activity of each enterprise was controlled by a national plan. Every enterprise was subsumed in a particular industrial sector—textile, chemical, food processing, and so on—and all industrial sectors were subsumed under the public sector controlled by the plan. Profitability played no role in the evaluation of the enterprise. What counted was the performance of the public sector as a whole. The net income of each enterprise was deposited in the National Treasury, which, in turn, allocated funds to the individual enterprises according to the plan. The plan was administered by a central organization that coordinated the accounts of the enterprises in each economic sector. Labor discipline and production were based on "conscience" and moral incentives.[50]

Guevara and his associates argued that their centralized budgetary system of finance could be implemented across the whole economy because of the relatively advanced system of communications and transport in the country that allowed for the effective coordination of economic activities on a national scale. Alexis Codina, an economic administrator under the jurisdiction of Guevara's ministry, claimed that the implementation of the system was also facilitated by the actual existence, in the island, of sophisticated accounting techniques—particularly in the large former US monopolies, such as the electric power and telephone utilities, as well as in the large corporations in the oil and the sugar sectors—that allowed for the kind of record keeping about inputs and outputs required by their system. However, those large enterprises were hardly typical of the non-sugar industrial enterprises run by Guevara's ministry. A study conducted by the Agricultural and Industrial Development Bank in 1954, five years before the revolutionary victory, listed 2,340 non-sugar industrial establishments, of which 78.6 percent showed the number of persons employed. Of these, 45.1 percent had fewer than five employees, while an additional 18.2 percent had from six to ten employees. Only 5.8 percent of establishments had more than a hundred employees.[51] Codina had to admit that those modern techniques were not evenly spread throughout Cuban industry. So, for example, in the consolidated flour industry that he administered, most of the enterprises lacked adequate accounting methods. Only a few factories employed them. Beyond these, a small number of smaller factories once used acceptable accounting systems, but ceased doing so after the revolution, among other reasons because the administrative and accounting personnel had left the country and there were no people trained to take over. The rest were workshops with a small number of laborers (*chinchales*), which had never even kept real books and had survived by bribing the tax inspectors when they came for inspections.[52] Codina noted that in order to incorporate these "chinchales" into the centralized budgetary system, the ministry had directly taken them over between 1961 and 1962 and had been administering them centrally through administrative subunits, which reduced the economic expense of having accounting personnel in each enterprise.[53]

Notwithstanding Codina's optimistic claims regarding the overall accounting methods in the Cuban industrial sector of the early 1960s, the annual state budgets that determined the necessary allocations ended up being prepared mostly based on primitive accounting techniques and were consequently a failure. The 1962 annual plan was prepared with the aid of Czech planners, but the figures for that plan were crudely estimated or invented, and there was no real input and feedback from lower echelons. Consequently production goals were too optimistic and had no basis in reality. When the final version of the plan came out, its gross miscalculations made it practically useless. Other centralized government plans for this period of the first half of the 1960s, sometimes made with the assistance of Soviet and Polish planners, fared no better. The lack of coordination among central ministries led to chaotic, unpredictable situations regarding the provision of inputs and the handling of outputs. Economic activity was hastily organized and staffed with inexperienced personnel operating in a freewheeling manner without control procedures. In addition, the political leadership kept interfering with the established plans by making economic decisions without consulting with the central planning board.[54] At best, Guevara's highly centralized system could have been applicable as the Cuban economist Joaquín Infante put it, in a more advanced economic stage than Cuba was in the early sixties,[55] thus underlining the objective limits to economic plans that Guevara was so inclined to play down, if not totally ignore.

When Guevara turned to the development and implementation of his extremely ambitious industrialization plan for Cuba, his centralized budgetary system ran into other problems. As the Canadian economist Archibald R. M. Ritter pointed out, the new industries selected for the plan were not suited to the capacity of the island. Programmed investment far exceeded absorptive capacity. Besides, the plans did not give sufficient attention or weight to the availability of raw materials or intermediate commodity inputs of Cuban origin. And, as it turned out, the new industries Cuba established were based on technologies mostly imported from the Soviet bloc that were already outdated in comparison with those of the advanced capitalist countries and even of prerevolutionary Cuba. The failure to discover and exploit significant reserves of oil in Cuban territory, which left no alternative but to import petroleum from the Soviet Union, delivered the final blow to Guevara's industrial plan.[56]

Estimates among Cuban and foreign scholars about the economic growth during the 1961–65 period vary widely, which the prominent Cuban economist Carmelo Mesa-Lago argued was connected to the lack of reliable data. Using scattered production data instead, Mesa-Lago concluded that there was either economic stagnation or decline in Cuba during this period.[57] In addition, Cuban gross national product figures did not register the widespread and considerable degradation of the quality of consumer goods, which was due in part to the exclusive emphasis on increasing the quantity of production. Thus, for example, inventories in women's and children's leather shoes more than doubled from January to August 1965, and dress inventories accumulated excessively because people refused to buy shoddy goods. The success indicators imposed on the Cuban enterprise by Guevara's plan stressed minimizing costs and increasing quantity, not the improvement of quality. In the case of shoes, the order to minimize costs was fulfilled by skimping on internal lining and thread, which reduced the average life of shoes from twelve to three months.[58]

Enterprise Self-Finance and the SDPE (System of Economic Direction and Planning)

The other side of the 1963–65 debate was represented by the policies of the Cuban INRA, which was in charge of the island's agriculture. It was supposed to follow the system of decentralized self-finance that had generally come to prevail in the Soviet Union and Eastern Europe during that time. Under that system, individual enterprises were considered legally independent. Each traded its products with other enterprises. Their success was determined by their profitability. They were expected to cover their current expenses through the banks that provided them with credit at a certain interest rate. Although these banks played a major role in controlling the enterprise, central agencies such as the treasury and planning ministries established overall aggregate limits or parameters.[59] Labor incentives were based on material rewards, although these were much more limited than in the Soviet Union and the Soviet bloc.[60] Thus, at their peak in 1985, all material incentives combined amounted to only 11 percent of worker income in Cuba, while they ranged from 15 percent of regular wages in Hungary to 36.4 percent in the Soviet Union and 55 percent in East Germany.[61] The INRA system, which had originally covered only the Cuban agricultural sector, came to dominate the whole economy from 1971 to 1985, a shift from 1966 to 1970, when Guevara's centralized model dominated the national economy. What had originally been the system adopted by INRA acquired its most elaborate form under the System of Economic Direction and Planning (SDPE) that was in force from 1976 to 1985, and was built around the five-year-plan model, with the first one implemented in the period between 1976 and 1980.[62]

However, government evaluations carried out in 1979, 1980, and 1985 revealed that the SDPE system was plagued by a number of serious flaws, some of which were characteristic of bureaucratic Communism elsewhere. A disconnection between producers and consumers led to problems such as shortages and poor quality of products, and a lack of producers' responsibility led to the over-demand for resources on the part of the plant managers who wanted to ensure they could fulfill their production quotas and consequently to the growth of idle resources in their enterprises. Following the same hoarding logic, more than one-third of the enterprises did not report inventories and half did not submit lists of unused inventories. As a result, some enterprises were shut down because they lacked the very supplies that sat unused in other enterprises. Contracts among enterprises often went unfulfilled, leading to delays and a chain reaction of bottlenecks. Because of price rigidities that prevented price reductions to clear accumulated merchandise, out-of-fashion and unattractive merchandise was stockpiled in inventories, and perishable goods were lost. Almost one-third of enterprises lacked quality controls in 1980, and 90 percent of the products did not meet quality standards approved by the Cuban government. Administrative personnel almost tripled between 1973 and 1984, which led to increased production costs and price increases.[63]

The same governmental evaluations also noted that the feedback and participation of lower echelons in the elaboration and control of the plan were poor, too formal, and relegated to minor issues.[64] This was a critical contradiction endemic to every Communist system, and that applied to the Cuban economy both under the system of self-financing of enterprises as well as to the budgetary system of finance. Under the conditions of complete political monopoly of the one-party state and mass media censorship, authentic feedback, truthful information, and independent initiatives from below were rare, if not altogether eliminated. In this situation, an institutionalized tendency develops for subordinates to tell their superiors what they want to hear, rather than the unpleasant truth about shortages of raw materials or the wrong replacement parts being sent to the factory. This is one of many systemic reasons that both these Cuban planning systems did not work well.[65]

Che Guevara and the Marxist Law of Value

The third principal aspect of the "great debate" of the 1960s was about the applicability of the law of value in the transition period from capitalism to communism. From a practical policy point of view, this was the least important of the three topics we have discussed here. However, it was quite central to Che Guevara's conception of the nature of socialism and communism. For Che, socialism meant the elimination of alienation, which was to be achieved through the abolition of competition and the market, as well as the abolition of the law of value through the establishment of central planning. For Guevara, this was a defining element of Marxism, not the replacement of the class power of the bourgeoisie by the economic and political power of the working class and its allies. In his words, "the law of value and planning are two terms linked by a contradiction and its resolution. We can say, then, centralized planning is the way of life of a socialist society."[66]

For classical Marxism, it is only under capitalism that most if not all products take the form of commodities. Only as commodities do products have exchange value, exchange value being an expression of the social relations between producers of commodities. It is, in fact, the only expression of the social character of labor in a society of independent producers. The law of value is the economic mechanism in a society of private producers, which distributes the total labor power at the disposal of society (and thereby all material resources necessary for production) between its various branches of production, via the mediation of the exchange of all commodities at their values. Under capitalism, this law determines the pattern of investment, that is, the inflow and outflow of capital in different branches of production, according to the deviation of their specific rate of profit from the average rate of profit.[67]

Under the conditions of a revolution in a less developed country such as Cuba, there were objective economic limits to the extent to which the law of value could be suppressed. One was the existence of substantial individual and family simple commodity production that could not be easily subjected to the directives of a central economic plan. In addition, at the time of the "great debate" from 1963 to 1965, Cuba was still to a considerable degree an open export-import economy subject to the vagaries of the world market.

Che Guevara, who adopted the classical Marxist conception of the law of value, was right to insist that the law of value should not be allowed to direct the destiny of a socialist economy. How else would industrial and agricultural workers be freed from having to work under the same conditions as under capitalism, to be guaranteed access to a number of basic goods independent of market-determined prices, and to begin planning to determine production and social priorities?[68]

However, Guevara also recognized that the law of value had to operate, if only partially, because of Cuba's highly developed foreign trade sector. He understood that the law of value governed commercial transactions even within the socialist camp and acknowledged that it also operated because elements of the mercantile society still remained. As an example, Che cited the type of exchange that took place between the state as a supplier and the individual consumer.[69] However, he did not mention the extensive simple production that existed in the country as an obstacle to central planning and how it helped to maintain the influence of the law of value in the island's economy. That is why, as Alexis Codina indicated, Guevara's Ministry of Industry tried to incorporate the chinchales in his central planning and administration.

While Guevara had denied that the relationship among state enterprises in Cuba was at all commodified, later, when he became more critical of the Soviet Union, he began to see capitalist tendencies there and argued that the state enterprises in the Soviet Union were selling means of production to each other as merchandise or commodities.[70] However, this was a mistaken interpretation of the prevailing situation in the Soviet Union in the first half of the sixties since the state enterprises were not truly independent entities regardless of their formal legal status and thus could not truly engage in the buying and selling to each other of merchandise or commodities. Even under the important reforms adopted in 1965, which had the declared intention of increasing managerial powers, the success of and bonuses granted to the managers still depended primarily on the fulfillment of the national plan.[71] Yet, in contradiction with this evaluation, Che wrote elsewhere in his *Apuntes* that there was no relationship in the Soviet Union between the regulated scale of internal prices and the scale of prices in the world market, a clear instance of the suppression of the law of value in the Soviet Union.[72]

For their part, supporters of the decentralized self-financing method, such as minister of foreign trade Alberto Mora (originally a major in the Directorio Revolucionario), argued that in a planned economy, the law of value does not disappear and that under socialism the law of value operates concretely in the making and implementation of the plan.[73] Implying that there was competition in Cuba's "socialist" society, Mora asserted that the state sector in Cuba did not constitute "a single large enterprise" since there were differences of opinion and conflicts among the various enterprises subsumed under it. Following Mora's approach, General Motors would not have been considered a single enterprise, since, like in any other large bureaucracy, there is no lack of backbiting and conflict among the various sectors of its managerial hierarchy. Fundamentally, however, Mora's conception of the law of value was very different from the classical Marxist concept. For Mora, the law of value was rooted in economic scarcity, not in the capitalist marketplace, as was the relationship between available resources and the growing needs of humanity. Therefore, he asserted, the law of value would cease to operate only when the development of the productive forces created enough resources to fully satisfy humanity's fundamental, or socially recognized, needs.[74]

What Was Not Debated

The "great debate" of 1963–65 was not only restricted to a small elite public, both in terms of participation and audience, but was also limited to economic questions that involved criticisms of the Soviet economic model by other Communist currents that fundamentally accepted the structures of the one-party state undemocratically controlling the whole economy from above. Basically it was a debate between two tendencies within the ruling group about the most effective way to get workers to be productive (material versus moral incentives) and about the most effective manner for state managers and administrators to organize enterprises (self-financing versus budgetary system of finance).[75]

The debate elided much more fundamental issues about the economy that were not open to even limited public discussion, much less popular consultation and decision-making, and were instead unilaterally decided by the Cuban government. The following fundamental issues would have been open to intense debate in the mass media, as well as in specialized publications, in any society with a legitimate claim to be both socialist and democratic:

- What proportion of the economy should be devoted to production of goods and services for immediate consumption, and what proportion should be saved for replacement and innovation for future consumption? Consequently, what wage policy should the government adopt?
- What should be the policy toward individual and family production—so widespread in Cuba—in the transition to socialism?
- What should be the role and conditions for foreign investment in what was, after all, an economically less developed country lacking investments in part because of the US economic blockade? What should be the policy of industrialization in light of an agricultural, and to a lesser extent mining (for example, nickel), export economy with one major market (the United States) closed for an indeterminate period of time?

It is interesting to note that Che had considered the role of popular participation in economic decision-making, but he did not refer to the concept of popular or worker's control, a notion with which he was certainly familiar, though in this context, he distinguished between the preparation of economic plans, including the rate of growth and types of production, and the implementation of those plans.[76] He thought that there should be broad mass participation in preparing economic plans but not in their implementation, since he expected that to become an "entirely mechanical and technical process."[77] In Guevara's view, such implementation of plans would render unions superfluous and would eventually make them disappear.[78] His views on this issue paralleled and were perhaps influenced by Edward Bellamy's *Looking Backward*, the influential North American utopian novel of the late nineteenth century. According to Orlando Borrego, Che's close collaborator and his informal literary and political executor, Guevara greatly admired Bellamy's work, even to the point of declaring that "it coincided with what we are proposing."[79] Bellamy's socialist utopia in *Looking Backward* is expressly modeled on the army as the ideal pattern of society—regimented, hierarchically ruled by an elite, organized from the top down, with the cozy communion of the beehive as the great end. All production-related issues have become a matter of purely administrative technique to be handled by administrators and experts who "know" all aspects of production. Universal suffrage is abolished and representative bodies of any kind, from unions at the production level to parties in the political realm, have been made irrelevant.[80]

The "Great Debate" and Cuban Economic Cycles

Until the collapse of the Soviet Union in the early 1990s, the Cuban government tended to alternate between the Guevaraist centralized model (implemented partially in 1961–65, and then nationwide in 1966–70 and 1986–90), and the Soviet self-financing model (partially in 1961–65 and throughout the national economy in 1971–85). The swings of the Cuban government from one model to the other were largely due to serious labor problems—including absenteeism, decline in hours worked, lack of skill, and carelessness—which the government attempted to resolve by resorting to either material or moral incentives, and sometimes even to coercion and the militarization of labor, in order to elicit a greater dedication to work among the Cuban people.[81] In addition, as in other Communist countries, the use of material and nonmaterial incentives in Cuba was also associated with other important economic policies. These may have included planning methods, the organization of the enterprises, allocation of resources, income equalization, and mass mobilization for economic purposes.[82] For example, the adoption of the Soviet model of self-financing enterprises in Cuba in the 1970s was accompanied by the adoption of material incentives, all of which resulted in the creation of a somewhat higher degree of unemployment and income inequality.[83]

Guevara's economic policy was implemented nationwide for the first time by Fidel Castro from 1966—when Guevara had already resigned from the Cuban government to undertake guerrilla warfare abroad—until 1970. The policy's emphasis on capital accumulation at the expense of consumption reached its high point. In other words, the large increase in national savings was achieved at the expense of consumption through the expansion of rationing, the exporting of products previously consumed at home, and the reduction of imports regarded as superfluous. The share of state investment funds going into production rather than consumption increased for the 1965–70 period from 78.7 percent to 85.8 percent, the highest proportion ever achieved during the revolutionary period.[84] Nevertheless, with the exception of a few agricultural and industrial products, the country experienced a general decline in economic output. The country's poor economic performance, combined with the pressure from the Soviet Union, which was subsidizing the Cuban economy, forced the government to abandon the Guevaraist system and adopt orthodox Soviet methods during the 1970s.

Guevaraist economic policies were again implemented during the "Rectification of Errors" period of 1986–90, in order to combat a number of ills that the government was facing, such as a considerable slackening of work effort, a virtual disappearance of volunteer labor, and nepotism.[85] The government increased output quotas and reduced material incentives—wages, bonuses, prizes, and overtime funds. It also revived unpaid voluntary work and labor mobilization and created new construction contingents while maintaining material incentives only in some areas of the economy such as tourism. While the government gave lip service to increased worker participation in production, it actually reinforced managerial control of the workforce.[86] This was a period of poor economic performance starting in 1986, the year Cuba stopped paying the debt it had contracted with the countries of the Paris Club. Figures published by the Cuban National Bank in 1995 show that the GDP for the 1986–90 period declined annually by 1.3 percent in absolute terms and by 2.3 percent in per capita terms. Exogenous factors such as drought, a decline in the world price of sugar, and deterioration in the terms of trade with the Soviet Union played a role in this decline. But the policies of the Rectification period itself, such as elimination of the private farmers' market, had a very negative effect too.[87] The collapse of the Soviet bloc and the USSR in the late 1980s and early 1990s brought the Rectification period and its economic policy to an end and delivered a huge blow to the Cuban polity and economy.

Such policy cycles and oscillations were not unique to the Cuban economy, however. In the case of China under Mao—with whom Guevara, by his own admission, shared certain political inclinations—the stress on "moral incentives" was associated with a process of sharply increasing investment that left fewer resources for consumption. As high investment and moral incentives increased, social dislocation and discontent grew among workers and peasants because of the absence of basic consumer goods and because of the ever-diminishing material rewards for increased work. Eventually, the regime was forced to grant certain concessions in the form of greater material incentives. This is what happened as a result of the government's Great Leap Forward of 1958–61. The regime was forced to abandon that campaign because of the lack of food and the resulting famine and death of millions of people, and poor morale, even in the army. The peasants were then encouraged to return to private plots and rural markets, and the Chinese government began to pay the workers piece rates and bonuses made possible by sharply reduced capital accumulation.[88]

The occurrence of comparable cycles in Cuba and China is an expression of the systemic features that characterize bureaucratic Communism. The economic failures and the unrest in periods of intense accumulation associated with Mao and Guevara (though mostly after he had left the government) were eased by somewhat less onerous forms of exploitation until the government felt confident enough to return to the "old ways" and resume its accumulation frenzy. Needless to add, the obvious differences between Mao's China and Castro's Cuba do not contradict their Communist systemic similarities.

A bureaucratic Communist ruling class has two basic mechanisms to increase labor productivity without converting a society to capitalism: introduce market mechanisms or highly voluntarist and/or highly repressive mobilizations of workers to work longer and harder for less. The more revolutionary versions of Communism such as the ultraleft Third Period Stalinism of the late twenties and early thirties (before the introduction of the more moderate Popular Front of the mid-thirties) and Mao's and Guevara's politics were associated with the voluntarist and repressive economic options that entailed greater accumulation at the expense of popular consumption. No wonder that a terminological inversion occurred in China especially after the Cultural Revolution where "leftism" became associated with party control of all aspects of life and greater political and economic oppression.[89]

At the same time, Third Period Stalinism, Maoism, and Guevaraism had a more aggressive and revolutionary attitude toward capitalism as they tried to spread their form of class rule to countries beyond their own. However, they could only succeed when revolutionary situations occurred in societies where the institutions of capitalist rule were very weak, mostly in the global South. Such was the fate of revolutionary Communism in the twentieth century.[90]

Conclusion

The Setting—Characteristics of the Cuban Revolution

Contrary to conventional wisdom and expectations, the Cuban Revolution showed that it was possible to make a successful revolution against US imperialism barely ninety miles from its shores. Even more unexpectedly, the revolution adopted a Soviet-style Communist socioeconomic and political system and had considerable popular support due to its anti-imperialist nationalist content, and until the early nineties it satisfied basic material needs for the majority of the people, although it was plagued by chronic shortages of many essential consumer goods. The revolutionary government also instituted a generous welfare state massively subsidized, due to a mixture of ideological and realpolitik imperialist interests, by the Soviet bloc.

Until the collapse of the USSR and Eastern European Communism at the beginning of the 1990s, the great majority of the Cuban people were able to maintain a standard of living that, although certainly austere, assured the satisfaction of basic needs, particularly regarding education and health. The removal of much of the economic insecurity of Cubans and the increase of their social mobility, partly caused by the departure of the upper class and a large proportion of the middle classes, cemented the social base for the new social system. At the same time, the regime thoroughly repressed every expression of organizational autonomy and opposition whether from the working class and oppressed groups or from anybody else. Moreover, the policy adopted by the United States in the early 1960s of encouraging the departure of Cubans from the island and welcoming them as refugees had the unanticipated effect, from the US government's point of view, of diminishing and undermining any potential resistance to the Cuban government.

Viewed from a comparative Communist perspective, the prerevolutionary predominance on the island of an agricultural proletariat more interested in improving its standard of living than on owning land greatly facilitated the large-scale state collectivization of agriculture after the revolution and also diminished potential resistance to the regime. The Cuban case also differed from other Communist revolutions because its revolution was not led by an official Communist Party but was carried out instead by a multiclass movement led by a declassed (in the sense that it had no strong organizational or institutional ties either to the petty bourgeoisie or to any of the country's major social classes) leadership group. That is why the founding congress of the ruling Cuban Communist Party did not take place until 1965, several years after Communism had been established on the island, although it should be noted that the PSP, the old pro-Moscow Communist Party, one of the political groups that came together to form the new Communist Party in 1965, did play an integral part of the Cuban revolutionary process, particularly after the triumph of the revolution.[1]

Che Guevara and the Cuban Revolutionary Leadership

The main leaders of the Cuban revolution—Fidel Castro, Raúl Castro, and Che Guevara—had different political leadership styles.[2] Fidel Castro, by far the most important leader, was, until he retired for health reasons in 2006, a charismatic and tactically shrewd revolutionary politician, intent on consolidating his power, and initially averse to risking a loss of control of the island because of a premature implementation of ideological goals. Second in command was Fidel's younger brother, Raúl, who quickly acquired a reputation for his repressive activities as well as for his organizational discipline and skills.[3] Raúl was a former member of the Socialist Youth, the youth group of the Cuban Popular Socialist Party (PSP), but was still sympathetic to the Soviet Union. Then there was Che Guevara, whose iconic image has survived the collapse of the USSR and the decline of Cuban Communism. In some ways, almost fifty years after his murder, Che has emerged as the most important of the three leaders. Yet, as I have argued, Che Guevara's politics had far more in common with the politics of the Castro brothers than many of his current admirers would care to admit. First, he shared with them a revolutionary politics from above that allowed him to retain, along with the Castros, the political control and initiative on the island, based on a monolithic conception of a type of socialism immune to any democratic control and initiative from below.[4] Like the Castro brothers, Guevara had a deep commitment to the one-party state and to an extreme version of vanguardism, which he sometimes took to the level of absurdity. For example, his response to the social and political conditions he found in the eastern Congo, which he himself acknowledged lacked any of the necessary conditions for socialist revolution—such as the demand for land on the part of the vast rural population, a working class (which did exist in the Katanga region), and a significant imperialist presence that could provoke a sentiment of national resistance—was to create a vanguard Communist Party that would singlehandedly lead the revolution in that part of the country.

As early as the days of the guerrilla struggle in the Sierra Maestra, Guevara explicitly articulated the conception of the Cuban revolutionary leaders assigning a supportive and subordinate role in the revolution to the working class and the peasantry. Years later, when he was leading his small guerrilla forces in Bolivia, he subordinated the needs and political potential of the militant and politically conscious Bolivian workers to those of the very small guerrilla forces under his command. Even when he occasionally referred to the working class as playing a role in the seizure of power, he did so in deference to the putative working-class ideology of the Communist Party, treating the working class only as an ideological abstraction. Later on, after he left the Cuban government to engage in guerrilla warfare abroad, he deepened his commitment to a perspective that placed technological autonomy and determinism—not the working class—at the center of the socialist economy in a manner reminiscent of Edward Bellamy's utopian *Looking Backward*, a novel that he greatly admired.

The Idiosyncracies of Che Guevara

But Che Guevara also differed from the Castro brothers in some important respects. He was a radical egalitarian, a trait that was rooted in his bohemian upbringing in Argentina. His almost six years in power in Cuba (1959–65) did not diminish this trait at all. This was also the case with his political honesty, particularly in comparison with the very manipulative Fidel Castro. He also had a profoundly ascetic edge that led him, for example, to try to impose, in contrast to other revolutionary leaders, puritanical policies during his occupation of the town of Sancti Spiritus in central Cuba in 1958, and to consider, in a meeting of the Ministry of Industry that he directed, that the development of "consciousness" could reverse material progress in consumer goods. According to Guevara, the Cuban people could be educated to do without television altogether, based on the example of the Vietnamese, who did not have television and were nevertheless building socialism.[5] Guevara's internationalism or, more precisely, his willingness to spread the revolution outside of the island, particularly to the rest of Latin America, was more pronounced than that of the Castro brothers. Nevertheless, it was based on a clear ultra-vanguardism and the substitution of the working class and the peasantry by the Communist Party's "dictatorship of the proletariat," leading to the establishment of a new ruling class.[6] Che's egalitarianism and internationalism were also tied to a hypervoluntarism that expressed itself both in politics and in economic policy through his stress on moral incentives and creating a "New Man" who was totally dedicated to society and oblivious to his individual fulfillment.[7]

Guevara's personal and political characteristics—his political honesty and his radical egalitarianism—might have made him better suited to being a Communist oppositionist than a long-term Communist ruler who would have needed to live with the growth of inequality and corruption that has accompanied the Cuban Revolution. Although his egalitarianism, honesty, and asceticism might have helped to build and consolidate Cuba's Communist Revolution, the system he helped to build would almost certainly have turned against his most fundamental values. Max Weber famously argued that the ascetic Puritan ethic played a key role in the original development of capitalism, but that later, after "asceticism undertook to remodel the world and to work out its ideals in the world, material goods have gained an increasing and finally an inexorable power over the lives of men as at no previous period in history. Today the spirit of religious asceticism—whether finally, who knows?— has escaped from the cage. But victorious capitalism, since it rests on mechanical foundations, needs its support no longer."[8] The same might as well have applied to the Communism that Guevara helped build in Cuba.

The Common Goal

Notwithstanding the differences Guevara had with the Castro brothers and the Cuban pro-Moscow Communists, he shared with them, until the very end, the same project to overthrow capitalism and build a new socialist society. This shared project was based on the creation of a new class system based on state collectivism, a property form in which the state owns and controls the economy and a central political bureaucracy "owns" the state. Membership in the ruling class is determined by having a position in a bureaucracy that is at the center of power in a society and fuses political and economic powers. Such bureaucratic societies are characterized by the production of use values satisfying social needs that are determined by the ruling class. In this system, the surplus for the most part is not appropriated by the individual enterprise that produced the surplus, nor is it primarily realized through the market. Instead, it is appropriated by the state for the economy as a whole. The state appropriates this surplus through its mechanisms of planning and control—by determining what, how much, and where goods are produced. The surplus does not primarily go to fund the salaries and privileges of the bureaucrats (any more than profits go to primarily finance the private consumption of the capitalist class), though the state's officials may indeed enjoy special privileges. It goes first to fund accumulation and investment, defense, and other forms of spending as decided by the bureaucracy, and as the capitalists and the capitalist market do under capitalism. A critical contradiction exists in this social system between the need for planning and the absence of political freedom essential for efficient and accurate planning. Without political freedom, there is no authentic feedback, truthful information, and independent initiative from below that make it possible for economic plans to be carried out well.

Coda

The antibureaucratic rebels and revolutionaries who may have been inspired by the intransigent revolutionary spirit represented by Guevara's iconic image may attain their goals, as this study has tried to show, only through a process that brings together the politics of socialism, democracy, and revolution. Socialism: because the true liberation of working people can only be attained when both the economy and the polity come under the control of the women and men who through their work make social existence possible. Democracy: because majority rule and respect for minority rights and civil liberties is the only way that working people can in fact, and not in theory alone, control their destiny. Revolution: because even the most welcome, authentic reforms cannot bring about true emancipation and liberation. In any case, the resistance of the powerful to radical social change is likely to make revolution both unavoidable and desirable.

Acknowledgments

I want to thank Anthony Arnove, editor at Haymarket Books, who encouraged this project and provided me with editorial guidance. I am indebted and grateful to Dao X. Tran for her guidance in resolving numerous editorial problems. Thanks also to Ida Audeh, who proofread the book, and to the entire team at Haymarket Books: Nisha Bolsey, Rachel Cohen, Julie Fain, Rory Fanning, Jason Farbman, Eric Kerl, Jon Kurinsky, Jim Plank, John McDonald, Bill Roberts, Jesus Ramos, and Ahmed Shawki.

I am especially grateful to a number of people who have criticized and commented on various chapters: Guillermo Almeyra, Mel Bienenfeld, Stuart Easterling, Adolfo Gilly, Dan Labotz, and Charles Post. I am solely resposible for the views expressed in this book. Finally, I want to acknowledge the invaluable help provided by several faculty and staff members at the Brooklyn College Library.

To my wife, Selma Marks, I owe the deepest acknowledgment not only for her detailed and very valuable suggestions and criticisms of this work but for a lifetime of support, patience, and endurance. To her, my profound gratitude and love.

Selected Bibliography

Books and Pamphlets

Alarcón Ramírez, Dariel (Benigno). *Memorias de un soldado cubano*. Barcelona: Editorial Tusquets Editores, S.A., 1997.

Almeyra, Guillermo, and Enzo Santarelli. *Che Guevara. El pensamiento rebelde*. Mexico, D.F.: Ediciones La Jornada, 1997.

Anderson, John Lee. *Che Guevara: A Revolutionary Life*. New York: Grove Press, 1997.

Baez, Luis. *Secretos de generales*. La Habana: Editorial Si-Mar, 1996.

Barroso, Miguel. *Un asunto sensible*. Barcelona: Mondadori, 2009.

Bernardo, Robert. *The Theory of Moral Incentives in Cuba*. University: University of Alabama Press, 1971.

Besancenot, Olivier, and Michael Löwy. *Che Guevara: His Revolutionary Legacy*. New York: Monthly Review Press, 2009.

Bonachea, Ramón, and Marta San Martín. *The Cuban Insurrection: 1952–1959*. New Brunswick, NJ: Transaction Books, 1974.

Bonachea, Rolando E., and Nelson P. Valdés, eds. *Che: Selected Works of Ernesto Guevara*. Cambridge, MA: MIT Press, 1969.

Borrego, Orlando. *Che. El camino del fuego*. La Habana: Imagen Contemporanea, 2001.

Castañeda, Jorge G. *Compañero: The Life and Death of Che Guevara*. Translated by María Castañeda. New York: Alfred A. Knopf, 1997.

Chaliand, Gérard (ed. with an Introduction). *Guerrilla Strategies*. Los Angeles and Berkeley: University of California Press, 1982.

Constenla, Julia. *Celia: La madre del Che*. Buenos Aires: Editorial Sudamericana, 2004.

Debray, Régis. "Revolution in the Revolution? Armed Struggle and Political

Struggle in Latin America." Special issue, *Monthly Review* 19, no. 3 (July–August 1967).

Deutschmann, David, ed. *Che Guevara and the Cuban Revolution: Writings and Speeches of Ernesto Che Guevara*. Sydney: Pathfinder/Pacific and Asia, 1987.

Domínguez, Jorge. *Cuba: Order and Revolution*. Cambridge, MA: Belknap Press of Harvard University Press, 1978.

———. *To Make a World Safe for Revolution*. Cambridge, MA: Harvard University Press, 1989.

Draper, Hal. *The "Dictatorship of the Proletariat" from Marx to Lenin*. New York: Monthly Review Press, 1987.

———. *Socialism from Below*. Edited by E. Haberkern. Atlantic Highlands, NJ: Humanities Press, 1992.

Engels, Friedrich. *Socialism: Utopian and Scientific*. Translated by Edward Aveling. New York: Pathfinder, 1972.

Farber, Samuel. *Before Stalinism: The Rise and Fall of Soviet Democracy*. New York: Verso; Cambridge: Polity Press, 1990.

———. *Cuba Since the Revolution of 1959: A Critical Assessment*. Chicago: Haymarket Books, 2011.

———. *The Origins of the Cuban Revolution Reconsidered*. Chapel Hill: University of North Carolina Press, 2006.

———. *Revolution and Reaction in Cuba: 1933–1960*. Middletown, CT: Wesleyan University Press, 1976.

———. *Social Decay and Transformation: A View from the Left*. Lanham, MD: Lexington Books, 2000.

Fitzpatrick, Sheila. *Everyday Stalinism: Ordinary Life in Extraordinary Times: Soviet Russia in the 1930s*. New York: Oxford University Press, 2000.

Franqui, Carlos. *Diario de la revolución Cubana*. Paris: Ruedo Ibérico, 1976.

Fursenko, Aleksandr, and Timothy Naftali. *"One Hell of a Gamble": Khrushchev, Castro and Kennedy, 1958–1964*. New York: Norton, 1997.

Gadea, Hilda. *Ernesto: A Memoir of Che Guevara*. Translated by Carmen Molina and Walter I. Bradbury. Garden City, NY: Doubleday, 1972.

Gilly, Adolfo. *La senda de la guerrilla*. Ciudad México: Editorial Nueva Imagen, 1986.

Gleijeses, Piero. *Conflicting Missions: Havana, Washington and Africa 1959–1976*. Chapel Hill: University of North Carolina Press, 2002.

Gonzalez, Mike. *Che Guevara and the Cuban Revolution*. London: Bookmarks, 2004.

Guerra, Lillian. *Visions of Power in Cuba: Revolution, Redemption and Resistance, 1959–1971*. Chapel Hill: University of North Carolina Press, 2012.

Guevara, Ernesto Che. *The African Dream: The Diaries of the Revolutionary War in the Congo*. Translated by Patrick Camiller. New York: Grove Press, 2001.

———. *Apuntes críticos a la economía política*. Editado por María del Carmen

Ariet García. Ocean Press, 2006. [No place of publication]

———. *Escritos y discursos*. La Habana, Cuba: Editorial de Ciencias Sociales, 1977.

———. *Escritos económicos*. Cuadernos de Pasado y Presente, 5. Córdoba, Argentina: Cuadernos de Pasado, 1969.

———. *Guerrilla Warfare*. Translated by J. P. Morray. New York: Monthly Review Press, 1961.

———. *The Motorcycle Diaries: Notes on a Latin American Journey*. Melbourne: Ocean Press, 2004.

———. *Reminiscences of the Cuban Revolutionary War*. Melbourne: Ocean Press, 2006.

Guevara Lynch, Ernesto. *Young Che: Memories of Che Guevara by His Father*. Edited and translated by Lucía Alvarez de Toledo. New York: Vintage Books, 2007.

Hernández Otero, Luis, ed. *Sociedad cultural nuestro tiempo. Resistencia y acción*. La Habana, Cuba: Editorial Letras Cubanas, 2002.

Hoffman, David L. *Stalinist Values: The Cultural Norms of Soviet Modernity (1917–1941)*. Ithaca, NY: Cornell University Press, 2003.

Ibarra, Jorge. *Prologue to Revolution: Cuba, 1898–1958*. Translated by Marjorie Moore. Boulder, CO: Lynne Rienner, 1998.

Karol, K.S. *Guerrillas in Power: The Course of the Cuban Revolution*. New York: Hill and Wang, 1970.

Kidron, Michael. *Capitalism and Theory*. London: Pluto Press, 1974.

Lipow, Arthur. *Authoritarian Socialism in America: Edward Bellamy and the Nationalist Movement*. Los Angeles and Berkeley: University of California Press, 1982.

Loveman, Brian, and Thomas M. Davies, Jr. *Che Guevara: Guerrilla Warfare*. Wilmington, DE: SR Books, 1997.

Löwy, Michael. *The Marxism of Che Guevara: Philosophy, Economics, Revolutionary Warfare*. 2nd ed. Lanham, MD: Rowman & Littlefield, 2007.

Marot, John Eric. *The October Revolution in Prospect and Retrospect: Interventions in Russian and Soviet History*. Chicago: Haymarket Books, 2013.

Martínez-Fernández, Luis. *Revolutionary Cuba: A History*. Gainesville: University Press of Florida, 2014.

Mesa-Lago, Carmelo. *Cuba in the 1970s: Pragmatism and Institutionalization*. Albuquerque: University of New Mexico Press, 1974.

———. *The Economy of Socialist Cuba: A Two-Decade Appraisal*. Albuquerque: University of New Mexico Press, 1981.

———. *Market, Socialist and Mixed Economies, Comparative Policy and Performance: Chile, Cuba and Costa Rica*. Baltimore: Johns Hopkins University Press, 2000.

———, ed. *Revolutionary Change in Cuba*. Pittsburgh: University of Pittsburgh Press, 1971.

O'Donnell, Pacho. *Che: la vida por un mundo mejor*. Buenos Aires: Editorial Sudamericana, 2003.

Oltuski, Enrique. *Vida Clandestina: My Life in the Cuban Revolution*. Translated by Thomas and Carol Christensen. New York: Wiley, 2002.

Pérez-Stable, Marifeli. *The Cuban Revolution: Origins, Course and Legacy*. 2nd ed. New York: Oxford University Press, 1999.

Ramm, Hartmut. *The Marxism of Régis Debray: Between Lenin and Guevara*. Lawrence: Regents Press of Kansas, 1978.

Ritter, Archibald R. M. *The Economic Development of Revolutionary Cuba: Strategy and Performance*. New York: Praeger, 1974.

Silverman, Bertram (edited with an Introduction). *Man and Socialism in Cuba: The Great Debate*. New York: Atheneum, 1971.

Soria Galvarro T., Carlos. "Tomo 4 ¿Traición del PCB?" in *El Che en Bolivia. Documentos y testimonio*. La Paz, Bolivia: La Razón, 2005.

Stout, Nancy. *One Day in December: Celia Sánchez and the Cuban Revolution*. New York: Monthly Review Press, 2013.

Sweezy, Paul, and Leo Huberman, eds. *Régis Debray and the Latin American Revolution*. Special issue *Monthly Review*, 20, no. 3 (July–August 1968).

Sweig, Julia. *Inside the Cuban Revolution: Fidel Castro and the Urban Underground*. Cambridge, MA: Harvard University Press, 2002.

Taibo II, Paco Ignacio. *Ernesto Guevara también conocido como el Che*. Cuidad México: *Editorial Joaquín Mortiz*, S.A. de C.V., 1996.

Taibo II, Paco Ignacio, Froilán Escobar, y Félix Guerra. *El año que estuvimos en ninguna parte*. Ciudad México: *Joaquín Mortiz*, Planeta, 1994.

Waters, Mary Alice, ed. *The Bolivian Diary of Ernesto Che Guevara*. New York: Pathfinder, 1994.

Yaffe, Helen. *Che Guevara: The Economics of Revolution*. London: Palgrave MacMillan, 2009.

Articles

Childs, Matt D. "An Historical Critique of the Emergence and Evolution of Ernesto Che Guevara's Foco Theory." *Journal of Latin American Studies* 27, no. 3 (October 1995): 593–624.

Farber, Samuel. "The Cuban Communists in the Early Stages of the Cuban Revolution: Revolutionaries or Reformists?" *Latin American Research Review* 18, no. 1, (1983): 59–83.

———. "Material and Non-Material Work Incentives as Ideologies and Practices of Order." *Review of Radical Political Economics* 14, no. 4 (Winter 1982): 29–39.

———. "Raúl's Cuba." *Boston Review*, September/October 2013, http://www.bostonreview.net/world/cuba-raul-castro-reform-democracy.

———. "Reflections on 'Prefigurative Politics'." *International Socialist Review*

92 (Spring 2014): 78–91.

Kohan, Nestor. "Che Guevara, lector de *El Capital*. Diálogo con Orlando Borrego, compañero y colaborador del Che en el Ministerio de Industrias." *Rebelión*, 2 de julio del 2003, http://www.rebelion.org/noticia.php?id=51.

Shaikh, Anwar. "Foreign Trade and the Law of Value," Parts I and II. *Science and Society* 43, no. 3 (1979): 281–302 and 44, no. 1 (1980): 27–57.

Public Document

US Department of Commerce, Bureau of Foreign Commerce. *Investment in Cuba: Basic Information for United States Businessmen.* Washington, DC: US Government Printing Office, 1956.

Notes

To help readers find sources in Spanish, I have included those citations in Spanish.

Introduction

1. This perspective was best expressed, until recently, by *Espacio Laical*, the publication of the Félix Varela Cultural Center, sponsored by the Catholic Church. In June 2014, the Catholic hierarchy appointed new editors who have since substantially reduced the frequency of the journal and its political interventions. Meanwhile, the previous editors Roberto Veiga and Leinier González Mederos have created a new debate forum called "Cuba Posible," which has continued the editorial line and political orientation they previously followed in *Espacio Laical*.
2. For an overview of different tendencies in contemporary Cuban politics, see my article "The Future of the Cuban Revolution," *Jacobin*, January 5, 2014.
3. Samuel Farber, *Before Stalinism: The Rise and Fall of Soviet Democracy* (Cambridge and New York: Polity Press and Verso Books, 1990).
4. I use the terms *Communism* and *Communist* for the sake of clarity, simplicity, and convenience. However, as should be apparent from the content of this book, I do not link present-day Communism with the "classical" Communism of Marx, Engels, and many other revolutionaries who predate the rise of Stalinism. Furthermore, I also use *Communism* in a generic sense to describe a socioeconomic system, even though, of course, each Communist state has its own peculiarities and individual history. Marxists use the term *capitalism* similarly, despite the fact that capitalist states like the United States, Japan, and Sweden have significant differences.
5. Friedrich Engels and Karl Marx, "Rules and Administrative Regulations of the International Workingmen's Association (1867)," International

Workingmen's Association, https://www.marxists.org/archive/marx/iwma/documents/1867/rules.htm.

6. For a thorough account and analysis of the role of the urban revolutionaries in the struggle against the Batista dictatorship, see Julia E. Sweig, *Inside the Cuban Revolution* (Cambridge, MA: Harvard University Press, 2002).

7. Jorge G. Castañeda, *Compañero: The Life and Death of Che Guevara* (New York: Alfred A. Knopf, 1997), xv–xvi.

8. Rosa Luxemburg, "The Question of Suffrage," in *The Russian Revolution and Leninism or Marxism?* (Ann Arbor: University of Michigan Press, 1961), 64–65.

9. V. I. Lenin, *The Proletarian Revolution and Kautsky the Renegade*, in *Collected Works*, vol. 28, July 1918–March 1919 (Moscow: Progress Publishers, 1965), 255.

10. Farber, *Before Stalinism*, 122–24.

11. Luxemburg, "Question of Suffrage," 66.

12. For a thoughtful discussion of this and related questions, see the 2009 paper by Moshé Machover, "Collective Decision-Making and Supervision in a Communist Society," LSE Research Online, LSE Library Services, July 2013, http://eprints.lse.ac.uk/51148/.

13. "En tu cabeza hay una ametralladora, en mi cabeza hay política," entrevista a Mario Monje, http://www.taringa.net/posts/noticias/15509402/En-tu-Cabeza-hay-una-Ametralladora.html.

14. Inti Peredo, "En el banquillo. La deserción del P.C.," en *Tomo 4 ¿Traición del PCB? El Che en Bolivia, Documentos y Testimonios*, ed. Carlos Soria Galvarro T. (La Paz, Bolivia: La Razón, 2005), 142.

15. V. I. Lenin, "The Collapse of the Second International," http://www.marxists.org/archive/lenin/works/1915/csi/ii.htm.

16. Che Guevara, *Guerrilla Warfare*, trans. J. P. Morray (New York: Monthly Review Press, 1961), as reproduced in Brian Loveman and Thomas M. Davies, Jr., *Che Guevara: Guerrilla Warfare* (Wilmington, DE: SR Books, 1997), 50.

Chapter One

1. Jorge G. Castañeda, *Compañero: The Life and Death of Che Guevara*, trans. Maria Castañeda (New York: Alfred A. Knopf, 1997), 6.

2. Jon Lee Anderson, *Che Guevara: A Revolutionary Life* (New York: Grove Press, 1997), 57, 16, and Julia Constenla, *Celia: la madre del Che* (Buenos Aires: Editorial Sudamericana, 2004), 24, 31.

3. Constenla, *Celia: la madre del Che*, 95.

4. Castañeda, *Compañero*, 15.

5. Ibid.

6. Jon Lee Anderson, Guevara's biographer, uses the term *bohemian* with quotation marks to refer to the Guevara family. See Anderson, *Che Gue-*

vara, 20, 50. To be sure, radical leftist political activists in Argentina also rejected bourgeois cultural norms, but their focus and emphasis were political activism rather than the display of an alternative cultural lifestyle.

7. Thus, for example, the French novelist Gustave Flaubert expressed a bohemian sensibility when he saw the inability to understand certain forms of longing, the failure to aesthetically appraise the qualities of one's behavior, and the concern with the symbols of professional ambition as bourgeois. César Graña, *Bohemian Versus Bourgeois: French Society and the French Man of Letters in the Nineteenth Century* (New York: Basic Books, 1964), 183.

8. Che's parents got married on November 9, 1927, and Che was born on May 14, 1928. Even bohemian parents could not entirely ignore social pressures, and Che's official birthday was changed to June 14 so his parents could claim that he had been a premature baby. Constenla, *Celia: la madre del Che*, 19–21.

9. Anderson, *Che Guevara: A Revolutionary Life*, 39.

10. Constenla, *Celia: la madre del Che*, 62, 64.

11. Ibid., 54.

12. Pacho O'Donnell, *Che: la vida por un mundo mejor* (Buenos Aires: Editorial Sudamericana, 2003), 28.

13. Anderson, *Che Guevara: A Revolutionary Life*, 20.

14. Ibid., 18–19.

15. Paco Ignacio Taibo II, *Ernesto Guevara también conocido como el Che* (Mexico D.F.: Editorial Joaquín Mortiz, S.A. de C.V., 1996), 27; Castañeda, *Compañero*, 40; and Anderson, *Che Guevara: A Revolutionary Life*, 55.

16. Guevara's childhood friend Tatiana Quiroga portrayed him in his youth as a "hippyish and sickly figure." Anderson, *Che Guevara: A Revolutionary Life*, 67.

17. Ibid., 67, 36.

18. Constenla, *Celia: la madre del Che*, 155. These attitudes were long lasting, as when many decades later Che would contemptuously refer to the prominent gay Cuban playwright Virgilio Piñeira as a "*maricón*" (faggot) when he saw one of his books at the Cuban embassy in Algiers in 1963. Juan Goytisolo, *En los reinos de taifa* (Barcelona: Seix Barra, 1986), 174–75.

19. Anderson, *Che Guevara: A Revolutionary Life*, 50.

20. Ibid., 34.

21. Taibo, *Ernesto Guevara también conocido como el Che*, 29, 39.

22. Guevara was soon to explicitly reject nonviolence (not that he ever adopted it) as the road to political and social change, a view that he would reiterate on the occasion of his visit, as a representative of the Cuban government, to India and to Gandhi's tombstone, in the summer of 1959. Taibo, *Ernesto Guevara también conocido como el Che*, 363.

23. Castañeda, *Compañero*, 33; Constenla, *Celia: la madre del Che*, 74.

24. Anderson, *Che Guevara: A Revolutionary Life*, 49. According to Jorge Beltrán, a friend from Guevara's youth, Guevara had a different view from that of their liberal and strongly anti-Peronista parents. Although he was disgusted by the demagoguery, the lack of public liberties, and the economic corruption of Peronism, like so many others he valued the social programs of Evita and Juan Perón. O'Donnell, *Che: la vida por un mundo mejor*, 42.

25. Castañeda, *Compañero*, 23.

26. A couple of decades later when he was already a leading figure of the Cuban government, Guevara adopted a much more positive attitude and interest in Perón. Thus, he sent Jorge "Papito" Serguera, Cuba's first ambassador to Algeria, to see Perón during his years of exile in Spain and even went to visit him in the Spanish capital in 1965. O'Donnell, *Che: la vida por un mundo mejor*, 300, 408.

27. Castañeda, *Compañero*, 48.

28. Anderson, *Che Guevara: A Revolutionary Life*, 114.

29. Ernesto Che Guevara, *The Motorcycle Diaries: Notes on a Latin American Journey* (Melbourne: Ocean Press, 2004), 78.

30. Ernesto Guevara Lynch, *Young Che: Memories of Che Guevara by His Father*, ed. and trans. Lucía Alvarez de Toledo (New York: Vintage Books, 2007), 212, 218.

31. Anderson, *Che Guevara: A Revolutionary Life*, 163, 165.

32. Ibid., 63, 76–78.

33. Cited in Castañeda, *Compañero*, 59.

34. Cited in Anderson, *Che Guevara: A Revolutionary Life*, 120.

35. Ibid.

36. I am borrowing the notion of "domain assumptions" from the sociologist Alvin Gouldner, who posited that all social theories have an "infrastructure" consisting of several "domain assumptions" learned by individuals before they became social scientists, which, although not a part of the theory, leave an indelible mark upon it. These might include, for example, fundamental assumptions about human rationality and whether social problems might correct themselves without planned intervention. Alvin Gouldner, *The Coming Crisis of Western Sociology* (New York: Basic Books, 1970) and John K. Rhoads, "On Gouldner's Crisis of Western Sociology," *American Journal of Sociology* 78, no. 1 (July 1972): 136–54.

37. It is worth noting that this conception of the bourgeois revolutions failed to realize that these revolutions were usually fought by the popular classes rather than by the bourgeoisie, and that far from being an inevitable product of these revolutions, most individual and democratic rights had actually been achieved through subsequent working-class and popular struggles.

38. Norton Ginsberg, *Atlas of Economic Development* (Chicago: University of Chicago Press, 1961), 18.

39. This involved an average of twelve indexes covering such items as the

percentage of the labor force employed in mining, manufacturing, and construction; percentage of literate persons; and per capita electric power, newsprint, and caloric food consumption. Pedro C. M. Teichert, "Analysis of Real Growth and Wealth in the Latin American Republics," *Journal of Inter-American Studies* 1 (April 1959): 184–85.

40. It is significant that in Cuba and Argentina the Spanish word *bohemio* refers to the lifestyle of people who have irregular work hours (such as many journalists and artists) and who spend some of their nighttime hours at public venues like bars and restaurants. Thus, the term has no connotation of nonconformity or rebellion against bourgeois cultural and social norms.

41. Guevara Lynch, *Young Che*, 306; and Anderson, *Che Guevara: A Revolutionary Life*, 129.

42. Anderson, *Che Guevara: A Revolutionary Life*, 139. Ñico López was a member of the July 26th movement, who had previously been, like Raúl Castro, a member of the Juventud Socialista, the youth wing of the PSP, the Cuban Communist Party. He was murdered by Batista's army when he was captured shortly after the rebel landing in eastern Cuba in late 1956.

43. This was the name of the boat that took Fidel Castro and eighty-one other revolutionaries to Cuba in November 1956.

44. Ramón Guerra Díaz, "La Sociedad Cultural Nuestro Tiempo," monografias.com, June 18, 2013, http://blogs.monografias.com/cultura-cuba/2013/06/18/la-sociedad-cultural-nuestro-tiempo/.

45. Luis Hernández Otero, ed., *Sociedad Cultural Nuestro Tiempo: Resistencia y Acción* (La Habana, Cuba: Editorial Letras Cubanas, 2002), 159.

46. Ibid., 7, 25, 115. This term suggested among other things lack of patriotism and was not used in Cuba except by those influenced by the USSR. In that country, the term was commonly used as a sign of opprobrium, as when Stalin accused Soviet Jews of being "rootless cosmopolitans."

47. Hilda Gadea, Guevara's first wife, claimed that Che's adherence to Freudian psychology and Sartrean existentialism softened as his interpretations gradually became more Marxist. Anderson, *Che Guevara: A Revolutionary Life*, 131. For Guevara's critical view of socialist realism, see Ernesto Che Guevara, *Socialism and Man in Cuba*, in *Che: Selected Works of Ernesto Guevara*, eds. Rolando E. Bonachea and Nelson P. Valdés (Cambridge, MA: MIT Press, 1969), 165.

48. They were also not connected to working-class organizations. While many of Fidel Castro's associates had working-class backgrounds, very few of them had participated in working-class struggles. It must be noted that some of the leaders of the July 26th movement outside of Fidel Castro's group of close associates in the Sierra Maestra did have close links to organizations led primarily by middle-class people. This was the case of Frank País, who, with his parents and other members of his family, was very active in the life of the Baptist church. Moreover, it was not uncommon

for rank-and-file militants of the July 26 movement to be active in Catholic youth organizations and especially in the Masonic youth group AJEF (Asociación Juvenil Esperanza de la Fraternidad, Hope of the Fraternity Youth Association).

49. Anderson, *Che Guevara: A Revolutionary Life*, 185. One wonders how Che Guevara would have reacted had he known that Celia Sánchez, Fidel Castro's principal aide and companion, shortly after the victory of the revolution went to El Encanto, Havana's most famous and elegant department store, and bought herself four dresses and several pairs of high-heel shoes with pointed toes. As her sympathetic biographer notes, she subsequently turned up looking delicate, lovely, and expensive. Nancy Stout, *One Day in December: Celia Sánchez and the Cuban Revolution* (New York: Monthly Review Press, 2013), 331–32.

50. Hilda Gadea, *Ernesto: A Memoir of Che Guevara*, trans. Carmen Molina and Walter I. Bradbury (Garden City, NY: Doubleday, 1972), 155.

51. The assumption of the Nicaraguan poet Ernesto Cardenal that consumer goods such as soap were restricted to the Cuban middle classes is entirely without foundation, at least in urban areas. It is true that middle- and upper-class people were more likely to buy the finer kinds of toiletries that were usually, but not always, imported. Instead, urban working-class families were more likely to purchase the "coarser" domestic products and, if necessary, use rough and very inexpensive goods such as "Candado" soap, designed for washing clothes, for personal hygiene. For Cardenal's reflections on this matter, see Taibo, *Ernesto Guevara también conocido como el Che*, 404.

52. Ibid.

53. Minutes of the bimonthly meeting of the managers of the Ministry of Industry (MININD) on February 22, 1964, are noted in Ernesto Che Guevara, *Apuntes críticos a la economía política*, editado por María del Carmen Ariet García (Ocean Press, 2006), 304. [No place of publication was provided.]

54. For an example of Che Guevara's explicit invocation of the figure of Don Quijote, see "Letter to His Parents," in *Che: Selected Works of Ernesto Guevara*, 422.

Chapter Two

1. Maurice Zeitlin and Robert Scheer, *Cuba: Tragedy in Our Hemisphere* (New York: Grove Press, 1963), 207.

2. John Lee Anderson, *Che Guevara: A Revolutionary Life* (New York: Grove Prees, 1997), 139.

3. Jorge G. Castañeda, *Compañero: The Life and Death of Che Guevara*, trans. María Cantañeda (New York: Alfred A. Knopf, 1997), 62, and Anderson, *Che Guevara*: 167.

4. Castañeda, *Compañero*, 181, and Anderson, *Che Guevara: A Revolution-*

ary Life, 167.

5. Anderson, *Che Guevara: A Revolutionary Life*, 697.

6. Even the Cuban writer Leonardo Padura, the author of *The Man Who Loved Dogs*, who is certainly very knowledgeable about Leon Trotsky, asserted that "if there had been an appearance of Trotsky in Cuba, that would have been the Argentinian [Che Guevara]." Horacio Bilbao, "Si hubiera habido un asomo de Trotsky en Cuba, hubiera sido el Che," interview with Leonardo Padura, *Feria del Libro 2013*, 8 de mayo del 2013.

7. Guevara's close aide Orlando Borrego relates that he had difficulty joining the Cuban Communist Party because he was known to read the daily bulletin published by the official Chinese news agency. Guevara admonished those objecting to Borrego's membership application, telling them that should be a reason to congratulate rather than criticize Borrego and that Communists should read everything including the writings of the enemy. Nestor Kohan, "Che Guevara, lector de *El Capital*. Diálogo con Orlando Borrego, compañero y colaborador del Che en el Ministerio de Industrias," *Rebelión*, 2 de julio del 2003, http://www.rebelion.org/noticia.php?id=51.

8. A parallel can perhaps be drawn between Guevara and Felix Dzerzhinsky (Iron Felix), who died in 1926 at the age of forty-nine, before Stalinism had completely succeeded and consolidated itself. Although known for his often arbitrary repressive activities as the head of the Cheka, the Soviet secret police, Dzerzhinsky was also thought to be an honest and principled Communist.

9. Anderson, *Che Guevara: A Revolutionary Life*, 470, 605.

10. I want to thank Dan LaBotz for this insight as well as for other suggestions and criticisms of this chapter.

11. Karl Marx, *The Eighteenth Brumaire of Louis Bonaparte* (Moscow: Foreign Languages Publishing House, n.d.), 15.

12. For an articulate presentation of Communist parties in various parts of the world as reformist, see Ian Birchall, *Workers Against the Monolith: The Communist Parties since 1943* (London: Pluto Press, 1974). The works of other authors such as André Gunder Frank and Régis Debray also tended to suggest that the traditional Communist parties were not revolutionary.

13. Earl Browder made the serious mistake of wanting to continue the previous moderate Soviet line of amity with the United States and the allies beyond the time the Soviet Union considered it appropriate.

14. Some Cuban Communist leaders such as Aníbal Escalante broke with Fidel Castro, first because of their organizational sectarianism and later because of their admiration for the more prudent Soviet economic practices, but not because they were "reformists" and opposed Cuba's move toward Communism.

15. For a more detailed analysis of the old Cuban Communist Party and the question of whether it was reformist or revolutionary, see my article

"The Cuban Communists in the Early Stages of the Cuban Revolution: Revolutionaries or Reformists?" *Latin American Research Review* 18, no. 1 (1983): 59–83.

16. It is worth noting that Guevara's plan overlapped with Mao's "Great Leap Forward" in China (1958–61), an economic strategy that resulted in widespread famine and the death of millions of people.

17. Cited by Jorge Domínguez, *Cuba: Order and Revolution* (Cambridge, MA: Belknap Press of Harvard University Press, 1978), 383.

18. Castañeda, *Compañero*, 212.

19. Ibid., 213.

20. Cited in ibid., 216.

21. Carmelo Mesa-Lago, *The Economy of Socialist Cuba: A Two-Decade Appraisal* (Albuquerque: University of New Mexico Press, 1981), 16–17.

22. Castañeda, *Compañero*, 129, and Anderson, *Che Guevara, A Revolutionary Life*, 347.

23. Enrique Oltuski, *Vida Clandestina: My Life in the Cuban Revolution*, trans. Thomas and Carol Christensen (New York: Wiley, 2002), 199.

24. It is worth noting that the principal source of recruitment for the July 26th movement was the youth wing of the Partido Ortodoxo, of which Fidel Castro had been a member and congressional candidate, that had made a central plank of the struggle its opposition to the massive theft of public funds by the governments that preceded Batista and related phenomena such as the political gang warfare of the late 1940s and early 1950s.

25. Ernesto Che Guevara, "A Betrayal in the Making. July 1957," in Ernesto Che Guevara, *Reminiscences of the Cuban Revolutionary War* (Melbourne: Ocean Press, 2006), 119–26. For the text of the Sierra Maestra Manifesto, see Rolando E. Bonachea and Nelson P. Valdés, "Revolutionary Struggle 1947–1958," in *The Selected Works of Fidel Castro* (Cambridge, MA: MIT Press, 1972), 343–48.

26. Buró Obrero del II Frente Oriental "Frank País" in *Unidad y Acción* (Havana: Ediciones Verde Olivo, 1999), 55.

27. Partido Socialista Popular, "La Solución que Conviene a Cuba," December 10, 1958. This pamphlet, consisting of fifteen mimeographed pages, was obviously clandestinely produced. I read this pamphlet in the late sixties at the New York Public Library, which has a valuable collection of Cuban Communist publications.

28. It is worth noting that even Fidel Castro's more radical pronouncements in "History Will Absolve Me" (his defense speech at the trial for the assault on the Moncada Barracks on July 26, 1953), which was not much talked about in the socially moderate years 1956 to 1958, spoke about compensating the expropriated landlords.

29. Guevara, *Reminiscences of the Cuban Revolutionary War*, 10.

30. Ibid., 10–11.

31. A Guatemalan friend of Guevara's was excluded from the expedition not because, as Fidel Castro explained, "any negative attribute of his own, but because we did not wish to make of our army a mosaic of nationalities." Cited in Castañeda, *Compañero: The Life and Death of Che Guevara*, 88.

32. For a detailed account of the failed November uprising, the landing of the *Granma*, and subsequent events, see chapter 5 of Ramón Bonachea and Marta San Martín, *The Cuban Insurrection: 1952–1959* (New Brunswick, NJ: Transaction Books, 1974), 76–105.

33. Guevara, "Reinforcements: March 1957," in *Reminiscences of the Cuban Revolutionary War*, 65–69.

34. Paco Ignacio Taibo II, *Ernesto Guevara también conocido como el Che* (Mexico, D.F.: Planeta, Joaquín Mortiz, 1996, 188) and Carlos Franqui, *Diario de la Revolución Cubana* (Paris: Ruedo Ibérico, 1976), 362.

35. Castañeda, *Compañero: The Life and Death of Che Guevara*, 116–17, and Anderson, *Che Guevara: A Revolutionary Life*, 296–97.

36. As we shall see, Guevara's break with Moscow did not affect his continuing support for the fundamental political structures of the Communist one-party state.

37. Cited in Rolando E. Bonachea and Nelson P. Valdés, eds., *Che: Selected Works of Ernesto Guevara* (Cambridge, MA: MIT Press, 1969), 107.

38. Cited by Julia Sweig in *Inside the Cuban Revolution: Fidel Castro and the Urban Underground* (Cambridge, MA: Harvard University Press, 2002), 101.

39. Ibid.

40. Franqui, *Diario de la Revolución Cubana*, 611.

41. For an informative account of the background of a number of high-ranking Rebel Army officers, see Luis Báez, *Secretos de Generales* (Havana: Editorial Si-Mar, 1996).

42. Jorge Ibarra, *Prologue to Revolution: Cuba, 1898–1958*, trans. Marjorie Moore (Boulder, CO: Lynne Rienner Publishers, 1998), 170.

43. This was the case of the notorious Marcos Armando Rodríguez Alfonso "Marquitos," a PSP member who had infiltrated the DR. It was found, after the victory of the revolution, that he had betrayed the hiding place of leading members of the DR who were assassinated by Batista's police. "Marquitos" was tried and executed in 1964. For a very detailed analysis of the case, see Miguel Barroso, *Un asunto sensible* (Barcelona: Mondadori, 2009).

44. For an in-depth discussion of the role of the Cuban Communists and the Soviet Union in the Cuban Revolution, see chapter five, "The Role of the Soviet Union and the Cuban Communists," of my book *The Origins of the Cuban Revolution Reconsidered* (Chapel Hill: University of North Carolina Press, 2006), 137–66.

45. Bonachea and San Martín, *The Cuban Insurrection: 1952–1959*, 211–12.

46. Ibid., 218.

47. Jules Dubois, *Fidel Castro: Rebel – Liberator or Dictator?* (New York: New Bobbs-Merrill, 1959), 252, 254.

48. Sweig, *Inside the Cuban Revolution*, 150.

49. Ibid.

50. Ibid., 151.

51. Ibid., 152.

52. Che Guevara, *Guerrilla Warfare*, trans. J. P. Morray (New York: Monthly Review Press, 1961), as reproduced in Brian Loveman and Thomas M. Davies, Jr., *Che Guevara: Guerrilla Warfare* (Wilmington, DE: SR Books, 1997), 55–65, 81.

53. Ibid., 60. See also 116–17.

54. Ibid., 73.

55. Ibid., 72.

56. A number of women fought in the revolution against Batista and formed the "Mariana Grajales" platoon.

57. Guevara, *Guerrilla Warfare*, 112.

58. Ibid.

59. Ernesto Che Guevara, *The African Dream: The Diaries of the Revolutionary War in the Congo*, trans. Patrick Camiller (New York: Grove Press, 2001), 61.

60. Guevara, *Guerrilla Warfare*, 50.

61. Ibid., 72–73.

62. Ibid., 51.

63. Matt D. Childs, "An Historical Critique of the Emergence and Evolution of Ernesto Che Guevara's Foco Theory," *Journal of Latin American Studies* 27, no. 3 (October 1995): 613.

64. For a further discussion and analysis of this issue, see my works *Revolution and Reaction in Cuba, 1933–1960* (Middletown, CT: Wesleyan University Press, 1976) and *The Origins of the Cuban Revolution Reconsidered*.

65. "Notes for the Study of the Ideology of the Cuban Revolution," in Bonachea and Valdés, *Che: Selected Works of Ernesto Guevara*, 69.

66. See the case study of the Nicaraguan Revolution in Loveman and Davies, *Che Guevara: Guerrilla Warfare*, 364, 366.

67. "Guerrilla Warfare: A Method, " in *Che: Selected Works of Ernesto Guevara*, Bonachea and Valdés, 92–93.

68. "Message to the Tricontinental" in *Che: Selected Works of Ernesto Guevara*, Bonachea and Valdés, 177.

69. Richard Gott, "Introduction to Ernesto 'Che' Guevara," in Guevara, *African Dream*, xiii.

70. Piero Gleijeses, *Conflicting Missions: Havana, Washington and Africa 1959–1976* (Chapel Hill: University of North Carolina Press, 2002), 109–11.

71. Although the subtitle of the book describes it as "the diaries of the revolutionary war in the Congo," it is in reality a 244-page full-scale treatise

written after Guevara had left the Congo. Unlike the actual diaries that Guevara would later write in Bolivia, there are no daily entries anywhere in the book.

72. Guevara, *African Dream*, 1.
73. Ibid., 26, 49, 226.
74. Ibid., 11, 146, 198.
75. Ibid., 2.
76. Ibid., 52–54, 58, 174.
77. Ibid., 14–15. For a more extensive discussion of dawa and related matters, see Paco Ignacio Taibo II, Froilán Escobar, and Félix Guerra, *El año que estuvimos en ninguna parte* (Mexico D.F.: Joaquín Mortiz, Planeta, 1994), 51, 77–78, 130–32.
78. Ernesto "Che" Guevara, *The Motorcycle Diaries: Notes on a Latin American Journey* (Melbourne: Ocean Press, 2004), 161.
79. According to Victor Dreke, a Black Cuban officer who was Guevara's second in command. Testimony cited in Taibo et al., *El año que estuvimos*, 121.
80. Guevara, *African Dream*, 74–75.
81. Gott, "Introduction to Ernesto 'Che' Guevara," in Guevara, *African Dream*, xxiii.
82. Guevara, *African Dream*, 157.
83. Ibid., 230, 171.
84. Ibid., 221.
85. Ibid., 223–24.
86. When the Katangan Moise Tshombe in alliance with Belgium rose against Congolese leader Patrice Lumumba and had him murdered, the Organization of African Unity (OAU) supported the Cuban intervention in the Congo. Once the OAU managed to remove Tshombe from power, they wanted the Cubans to leave. Although the Cuban government initially resisted the African decision, they did eventually go along with it. Taibo et al., *El año que estuvimos*, 59, 213.
87. Guevara, *African Dream*, 240.
88. Ibid., 240–41.
89. Ibid., 241.
90. Ibid., 244.
91. See the farewell letter written by Che Guevara and read by Fidel Castro on October 3, 1965, in *Che: Selected Works of Ernesto Guevara*, Bonachea and Valdés, *Che*, 422–23.
92. Thus, for example, Pacho O'Donnell, a biographer of Guevara, claims that there were fifty Bolivians training in Cuba who could have been sent to reinforce Che's guerrilla foco, and that if the Cuban government had confirmed Che's presence in Bolivia, this would have generated a movement of leftist militants who would have gone to that country to help Guevara. Pacho O'Donnell, *Che: la vida por un mundo mejor* (Buenos

Aires: Editorial Sudamericana, 2003), 501.

93. For a more detailed development of this type of analysis, see chapter 3, "Cuba's Foreign Policy—Between Revolution and Reasons of State" in my book *Cuba Since the Revolution of 1959: A Critical Assessment* (Chicago: Haymarket Books, 2011), 96–130.

94. Castañeda, *Compañero: The Life and Death of Che Guevara*, 386.

95. K. S. Karol, *Guerrillas in Power: The Course of the Cuban Revolution* (New York: Hill and Wang, 1970), 491.

96. Dariel Alarcón Ramírez (Benigno), a Cuban peasant who joined the Rebel Army in the Sierra Maestra and was selected by Guevara to be part of the Bolivia group, claimed that the guerrillas only recruited one Bolivian peasant who had TB and was going to die soon anyway. Dariel Alarcón Ramírez, *Memorias de un soldado cubano* (Barcelona: Editorial Tusquets Editores, S. A., 1997), 158–59.

97. Mary-Alice Waters, ed., *The Bolivian Diary of Ernesto Che Guevara* (New York: Pathfinder, 1994), 223, 289.

98. Hartmut Ramm, *The Marxism of Régis Debray: Between Lenin and Guevara* (Lawrence: Regents Press of Kansas, 1978), 44, 101–2.

99. Loveman and Davies, *Che Guevara: Guerrilla Warfare*, 318–20.

100. Ramm, *The Marxism of Régis Debray*, 127–28. Pacho O'Donnell argues that the farm purchased in Alto Beni was too small and close to neighbors and was thus useless for training guerrillas. Furthermore, the press of events allowed little time to choose a better location and that is why Ñancahuazú was chosen. O'Donnell, *Che: La Vida por un mundo mejor*, 405.

101. Loveman and Davies, *Che Guevara: Guerrilla Warfare*, 318, 320.

102. Ibid., 319.

103. Waters, *The Bolivian Diary of Ernesto Che Guevara*, 171.

104. Ramírez (Benigno), *Memorias de un soldado cubano*, 155.

105. Ernesto Che Guevara, "What We Have Learned and What We Have Taught," December 1958, in *Che Guevara and the Cuban Revolution: Writings and Speeches of Ernesto Che Guevara*, ed. David Deutschmann (Sydney: Pathfinder/Pacific and Asia, 1987), 73.

106. It is interesting to note here that the Peruvian Hilda Gadea, Che Guevara's first wife, was a member of the left wing of APRA. He met her while they were both exiles in Mexico.

107. Guevara, "What We Have Learned," in Deutschmann, *Che Guevara and the Cuban Revolution*, 73.

108. Guevara, *Reminiscences of the Cuban Revolutionary War*, 56–58.

109. "Notes for the Study of the Ideology of the Cuban Revolution," in Bonachea and Valdés, *Che: Selected Works of Ernesto Guevara*, 51–52.

110. Waters, *The Bolivian Diary of Ernesto Che Guevara*, 289.

111. Ibid., 186.

112. Ibid., "Analysis of the Month" for July 1967, 244.

113. Second Declaration of Havana as cited by Ernesto Che Guevara in "Guerrilla Warfare: A Method," in Bonachea and Valdes, *Che: Selected Works of Ernesto Guevara*, 91.

114. Héctor Béjar, "The Failures of the Guerrillas in Perú," in *Guerrilla Strategies*, ed. Gérard Chaliand (Berkeley and Los Angeles: University of California Press, 1982), 288.

115. For V. I. Lenin's important writings on guerrilla warfare and its relationship to the Bolshevik and, more broadly, Russian social democratic politics, see his *Collected Works*, vol. 11 (Moscow: Progress Publishers, 1965), 213–23.

116. Contrary to the claims of some advocates of the "foco" theory that contrasted supposedly soft urban life with the rigors of guerrilla life in the hills, the much greater dangers of the urban underground in Cuba in fact forced hundreds of endangered activists to take refuge in the Sierra Maestra, while no rebels from the sierra were compelled to take refuge in the cities, except in the few cases of rebels who needed specialized medical attention.

117. US Department of Commerce, Bureau of Foreign Commerce, *Investment in Cuba: Basic Information for United States Businessmen* (Washington, DC: Government Printing Office, 1956), 183.

118. Guevara, *African Dream*, 241.

119. Ibid., 236.

120. Ibid., 240–41.

121. "Communiqué No. 5. to the Miners of Bolivia, June 1967," in *The Bolivian Diary of Ernesto Che Guevara*, Waters, ed., 312–14.

Chapter Three

1. Paco Ignacio Taibo II, *Ernesto Guevara también conocido como El Che* (Mexico D.F.: Editorial Joaquín Mortiz, S.A. de C.V., 1996), 354.

2. *Revolución*, February 16 and April 15, 1959.

3. For a more detailed discussion of this and related incidents, see my *Cuba Since the Revolution of 1959: A Critical Assessment* (Chicago: Haymarket Books, 2011), 22.

4. The trade-union "humanists" were seizing upon Fidel Castro's use of the term to distinguish his politics from those of capitalism and Communism during his visit to the United States in April 1959.

5. Jorge Ibarra, *Prologue to Revolution Cuba 1898–1958*, trans. Marjorie Moore (Boulder, CO: Lynne Rienner, 1998), 170.

6. Pacho O'Donnell, *Che: La vida por un mundo mejor* (Buenos Aires: Editorial Sudamericana, 2003), 205.

7. "Social Ideals of the Rebel Army," in *Che: Selected Works of Ernesto Guevara*, eds., Rolando Bonachea and Nelson P. Valdés (Cambridge, MA: MIT Press, 1969), 196–204.

8. "Interview by Telemundo Television," April 29, 1959, in ibid., 377.
9. The twenty-first-century reader in the economically developed capitalist democracies should keep in mind that we are not talking here about a small Communist opposition in a stable liberal democracy but about a political party, which in alliance with other forces, was a potential and credible contender for power in the context of a victorious revolution.
10. Traditional union-oriented social democracy was never a significant force in Cuba. Anarchism had been influential in the labor movement until the 1920s but sharply declined thereafter. Trotskyism had some influence in Cuba during the 1930s, but most of its adherents eventually merged into the populist Auténtico Party, and disappeared as a tendency. By the time of the 1959 revolution, Trotskyism had been reduced to a little-known, tiny group, except perhaps in a couple of towns and a handful of local unions in eastern Cuba. See Robert Alexander, *Trotskyism in Latin America* (Stanford, CA: Hoover Institution Press, 1973), 215–35.
11. For a listing of some of the unions under "unity" leadership, see the account of the labor rally at Parque Trillo in Havana during the summer of 1959 in "Denunció Jesús Soto el mujalismo que aún perdura en el movimiento obrero. Mitin en Parque Trillo," *Hoy*, July 6, 1959, 1.
12. See, for example, the report on May Day celebrations entitled "La unidad fue el centro de los discursos del Primero de Mayo" in *Hoy*, May 3, 1959. Majors Montseny and Gálvez gave "pro-unity" speeches in Santa Clara, and on the same day, Majors Raúl Castro and Che Guevara gave "pro-unity" speeches in Havana and Santiago de Cuba. It would not be farfetched to think that this "unity" milieu—in the army, trade unions, and elsewhere—could have become a source of opposition to Fidel Castro had the latter chosen to go in a political direction different from Communism.
13. Jon Lee Anderson, *Che Guevara: A Revolutionary Life* (New York: Grove Press, 1997), 384–85.
14. Ibid., 385.
15. Aleksandr Fursenko and Timothy Naftali, *"One Hell of a Gamble": Khrushchev, Castro and Kennedy, 1958–1964* (New York: Norton, 1997), 13.
16. Ibid., 11–12.
17. Ibid., 13.
18. Anderson, *Che Guevara: A Revolutionary Life*, 404, 406.
19. Fidel Castro's later claim that he had been a "Marxist-Leninist" by the time he took power is more likely to have been a retrospective self-validation of his membership in the Communist camp than a reliable historical account of his political evolution and history.
20. Tad Szulc, *Fidel: A Critical Portrait* (New York: Morrow, 1986).
21. Rufo López Fresquet, *My 14 Months with Castro* (New York: World,

1966), 111–12. Edward González also described several incidents indicating political tensions between Fidel Castro and Raúl Castro and Che Guevara in April and May 1959. See Edward González, "The Cuban Revolution and the Soviet Union, 1959–1960" (PhD diss., University of California at Los Angeles, 1966), 376–79.

22. For a detailed exposition of the relationship between the PSP, the Soviet Union, and Fidel Castro, see chapter 5, "The Role of the Soviet Union and the Cuban Communists," in my book *The Origins of the Cuban Revolution Reconsidered* (Chapel Hill: University of North Carolina Press, 2006), 137–72.

23. For details of this incident, see my *Cuba Since the Revolution of 1959: A Critical Assessment*, 40–41.

24. Euclides Vázquez Candela, "Saldo de una Polémica," *Revolución* (Havana), September 14, 1959, 1.

25. Anderson, *Che Guevara: A Revolutionary Life*, 429, 437, 440–41.

26. After he completed his sentence and went into exile in Miami, Huber Matos told English journalists that Che Guevara had been in communication with his relatives and told them that he did not approve of the death penalty for Matos, that he thought that the matter had been erroneously managed by Fidel Castro, and suggested that Matos's relatives should immediately appeal after the conclusion of the trial. Cited in Jorge G. Castañeda, *Compañero: The Life and Death of Che Guevara*, trans. Marina Castañeda (New York: Knopf, 1997), 144.

27. Taibo, *Ernesto Guevara también conocido como el Che*, 374–75.

28. Marifeli Pérez-Stable, *The Cuban Revolution: Origins, Course and Legacy*, 2nd ed. (New York: Oxford University Press, 1999), 72–73.

29. Law 962, August 1, 1961, in *Gaceta Oficial* (special edition), August 3, 1961, cited in Roberto E. Hernández and Carmelo Mesa-Lago, "Labor Organization and Wages," in *Revolutionary Change in Cuba*, ed. Carmelo Mesa-Lago (Pittsburgh: University of Pittsburgh Press, 1971), 212.

30. Ernesto Che Guevara, "The Working Class and the Industrialization of Cuba," in Bonachea and Valdés, *Che: Selected Works of Ernesto Guevara*, 243.

31. Ibid., 232–33.

32. Ernesto Che Guevara, *Revolución*, June 27, 1961, as cited by Hernández and Mesa-Lago, in "Labor Organization and Wages," in Mesa-Lago, *Revolutionary Change in Cuba*, 220.

33. Ernesto Che Guevara, *Apuntes críticos a la economía política*, editado por María del Carmen Ariet García (Centro de Estudios Che Guevara and Ocean Press, 2006), 412. Guevara also admitted in his *Apuntes* that union democracy in Cuba was a "perfect myth" since it was the Communist Party that proposed the single slate that got elected, with a greater or smaller vote, but without any mass involvement in the selection of the candidates (p. 413). However, Guevara drew no conclusions from his

admission about the political consequences of the one-party state.

34. Guevara, *Apuntes críticos a la economía política*, 249.

35. Guevara, "The Working Class and the Industrialization of Cuba," in Bonachea and Valdés, *Che: Selected Works of Ernesto Guevara*, 243.

36. Ibid.

37. René Dumont, *Cuba: Socialism and Development* (New York: Grove Press, 1970), 51–52 (Dumont's emphasis). The issue of Guevara's attitude toward workers' control is discussed at greater length in chapter 4.

38. Ernesto Che Guevara, "Discurso en la Convención Nacional de los Consejos Técnicos Asesores," in *Escritos y discursos* (Havana: Editorial de Ciencias Sociales, 1977), cited in *The Cuban Revolution*, Pérez-Stable, 102.

39. Ernesto Che Guevara, "Discusión colectiva: Decisión y responsabilidades únicas," in *Escritos y discursos*, cited in Pérez-Stable, *The Cuban Revolution*, 102.

40. Ernesto Che Guevara, "Discurso clausura del Consejo Nacional de la CTC, 15 de abril de 1962," in *Escritos y discursos*, cited in *The Cuban Revolution*, Pérez-Stable, 102.

41. Roberto E. Hernández and Carmelo Mesa-Lago, "Labor Organization and Wages," in Mesa-Lago, *Revolutionary Change in Cuba*, 221.

42. Ernesto Che Guevara in *Revolución*, February 2, 1963, cited in Hernández and Mesa-Lago, "Labor Organization and Wages," in Mesa-Lago, *Revolutionary Change in Cuba*, 220.

43. Anderson, *Che Guevara: A Revolutionary Life*, 134. Guevara also concluded on the basis of his Guatemalan experience that if that country's government had carried out executions, it would have had the possibility of hitting back at the opposition. Letter to his Argentinian friend Tita Infante as cited in Pacho O'Donnell, *Che: La vida por un mundo mejor*, 109.

44. V. I. Lenin, "How to Guarantee the Success of the Constituent Assembly," in *Collected Works*, vol. 25, June–September 1917 (Moscow: Progress Publishers, 1964), 382 (Lenin's emphasis).

45. V. I. Lenin, "Draft Resolution on Freedom of the Press," written November 4, 1917, in *Collected Works*, vol. 26, September 1917–February 1918 (Moscow: Progress Publishers, 1964), 283. For a fuller discussion and criticism of Lenin's views on the press under socialism and subsequent developments regarding freedom of the press in Soviet Russia, see chapter 3 "Freedom of the Press" in my *Before Stalinism: The Rise and Fall of Soviet Democracy* (Oxford: Polity Press and New York: Verso, 1990), 90–112.

46. Castañeda, *Compañero*, 103.

47. Ibid.

48. Anderson, *Che Guevara: A Revolutionary Life*, 237. Anderson goes on to comment that Guevara's chilling narrative reveals his personality, and that his matter-of-factness in describing the execution, and his scientific notations on his bullet's entry and exit wounds, suggest a remarkable

detachment from violence.

49. Castañeda, *Compañero*, 132. After the revolutionary victory, the revolutionary government, instead of abolishing the national lottery outright, transformed it into a savings plan as a transitional step toward its ultimate abolition.

50. Lillian Guerra, *Visions of Power in Cuba: Revolution, Redemption, and Resistance, 1959–1971* (Chapel Hill: University of North Carolina Press, 2012), 78–79. For a recent example of the serious accusations that have been leveled at Guevara for his conduct at La Cabaña, see María Werlau, "Las víctimas olvidadas del Che Guevara: ¿Cuántos fusilamientos están documentados? *Café Fuerte* (1 diciembre, 2014), http://cafefuerte.com/cuba/19698-las-victimas-olvidadas-del-che-guevara-cuantos-fusilamientos-estan-documentados.

51. Cited in Castañeda, *Compañero. The Life and Death of Che Guevara*, 178.

52. Helen Yaffe, *Che Guevara: The Economics of Revolution* (London: Palgrave Macmillan, 2009), 218.

53. Taibo, *Ernesto Guevara también conocido como El Che*, 485.

54. Yaffe, *Che Guevara: The Economics of Revolution*, 220–21.

55. As Yaffe claims in ibid., 216.

56. Daniel Bensaïd, *An Impatient Life: A Memoir* (London and New York: Verso, 2013), 165.

57. This is of course affected by circumstances such as whether revolutionary justice is being applied in a consolidated territory or in a moving front. In the latter case, the death penalty may be the only available punishment since a prison sentence would be meaningless in light of the brief and unstable control of territory by one side or another and the nonexistence of prisons.

58. This is an issue that came up in revolutionary Petrograd; some Bolshevik leaders proposed the "suppression of specific counterrevolutionary conspiracies" as opposed to the generalized terror proposed by other Bolshevik leaders. Alexander Rabinowitch, *The Bolsheviks in Power: The First Year of Soviet Rule in Petrograd* (Bloomington: Indiana University Press, 2007), 318. See also chapter 4 dealing with repression in my book *Before Stalinism: The Rise and Fall of Soviet Democracy*, 113–43.

59. For a lucid Marxist contribution to the question of revolutionary terror, see Hal Draper, Special Note C, "The Meaning of 'Terror' and 'Terrorism,'" in *Karl Marx's Theory of Revolution*, vol. 3: *The "Dictatorship of the Proletariat"* (New York: Monthly Review Press, 1986), 360–74.

60. Bensaïd, *An Impatient Life*, 166.

61. Even though it could be argued that Guevara might have used "man" here as a generic equivalent for "mankind," other writings of his, such as his treatise on guerrilla warfare discussed in chapter 2, suggest a more general political problem of gender bias. *Socialism and Man in Cuba* was actually a long letter Che Guevara wrote to Carlos Quijano, editor of

Marcha, a left-wing Uruguayan publication, in March 1965. The letter was published in Cuba in *Verde Olivo*, the Cuban army's newspaper, on April 11, 1965, and has been reproduced in many languages and editions. I am using the version that appeared in Rolando E. Bonachea and Nelson P. Valdés's *Che: Selected Works of Ernesto Guevara*, 155–69.

62. Orlando Borrego, *Che: el camino del fuego* (La Habana: Imagen Contemporanea, 2001), 378.

63. Guevara's "new man" is remarkably similar to the "new Soviet person," devoid of egotism and selfishness and ready to sacrifice personal interests for the sake of the collective that Stalin tried to create in the Soviet Union. David L. Hoffman, *Stalinist Values: The Cultural Norms of Soviet Modernity (1917–1941)* (Ithaca, NY: Cornell University Press, 2003), 15–56; see also Sheila Fitzpatrick, *Everyday Stalinism: Ordinary Life in Extraordinary Times in Soviet Russia in the 1930s* (New York: Oxford University Press, 1999), 75–79.

64. Guevara, *Socialism and Man in Cuba*, in Bonachea and Valdés, *Che: Selected Works of Ernesto Guevara*, 167.

65. Ibid., 163.

66. Ernesto Che Guevara, "Discurso pronunciado en la entrega de premios a obreros más destacados del mes de julio," published in *Hoy*, September 15, 1962, cited in *Che Guevara: Economics and Politics in the Transition to Socialism*, ed. Carlos Tablada (New York: Pathfinder, 1990), 178.

67. Guevara, *Socialism and Man in Cuba*, in Bonachea and Valdés, *Che: Selected Works of Ernesto Guevara*, 159.

68. Ibid.

69. Ibid., 163.

70. It seems that Che Guevara also had other difficulties with Marx's "Critique of the Gotha Program." Thus, in his *Apuntes* written between 1965 and 1966 he argues that the distribution according to work cannot be clearly established because all of the deductions that have to be made from the results of production for nonproductive activities such as social welfare expenditures. However, that is hardly a convincing objection since Marx was clearly arguing for a distribution to work *after* all the deductions from production were made. See Guevara, *Apuntes críticos a la economía política*, 340–42.

71. For a detailed description and analysis of the system of "popular power" established in Cuba in the 1970s, see my *Cuba Since the Revolution of 1959*, 29–31.

72. Bonachea and Valdés, *Che: Selected Works*, 157.

73. Guevara, *Socialism and Man in Cuba*, in ibid.

74. An authentic plebiscite suggests a secret vote in which the entire population of a region or country is asked to vote yes or no on a specific policy proposal. A true plebiscite also means that those opposed to the government's position can politically organize and campaign against it.

75. Let us look at an example of the abuse and misuse of the "dialectic" in Castro's Cuba. It was discovered in 1964 that PSP member Marcos Armando Rodríguez ("Marquitos") had infiltrated the Directorio Revolucionario during the struggle against Batista and betrayed the four leaders of that organization to Batista's police, who then immediately killed them. Since this revelation threatened the "unity" with the PSP, Fidel Castro tried to downplay Marquitos's spying activities inside the DR, arguing that his behavior should be viewed "dialectically," implying that the political conditions prevailing in 1964 had somehow changed the moral and political meaning of his 1957 spying. Miguel A. Barroso, *Un asunto sensible* (Barcelona: Mondadori, 2009), 186. The first time I became acquainted with the "dialectic," I had just graduated from a public high school near Havana and heard the word from a member of the Juventud Socialista (the youth wing of the PSP, the Cuban Communists) to justify the Soviet invasion of Hungary to crush the 1956 revolution in that country.

76. Guevara, *Socialism and Man in Cuba*, 162.

77. For a strong critique of informality as an obstacle to democracy, see Jo Freeman, "The Tyranny of Structurelessness," JoFreeman.com, n.d., www.jofreeman.com/joreen/tyranny.htm.

78. Ernesto Che Guevara, *Socialism and Man in Cuba*, in Bonachea and Valdés, *Che: Selected Works of Ernesto Guevara*,166–67.

79. Ibid., 167.

80. Ibid., 161.

81. Ibid., 167.

82. Ernesto Che Guevara, *The African Dream: The Diaries of the Revolutionary War in the Congo* (New York: Grove Press, 2001), 234.

83. Ernesto Che Guevara, "Message to the Tricontinental" (April 1967) in Bonachea and Valdés, *Che: Selected Works of Ernesto Guevara*, 180.

84. Taibo, *Ernesto Guevara también conocido*, 468. The issue of what aspects of the Soviet model Guevara rejected toward the end of his life is examined at greater length in chapter 4. We should also keep in mind that while Che never looked at China with the blind faith he had originally placed in the Soviet Union, he did occasionally consider it a possible model.

85. Che Guevara, *Guerrilla Warfare*, trans. J. P. Morray, originally published by Monthly Review Press in 1961, and reproduced in *Guerrilla Warfare*, 3rd ed. with revised and updated introduction and case studies, Brian Loveman and Thomas M. Davies, Jr. (Wilmington, DE: SR Books, 1997), 108.

86. See chapter 4 for a discussion of the "Great Debate" (of which the great majority of the Cuban population was unaware) that Che Guevara had with a number of important Cuban and foreign figures about such economic matters as the budgetary system of finance, material, and moral incentives, and whether the law of value operated under socialism.

87. "Con unidad monolítica Cuba seguirá adelante, dijo Raúl Castro,"

Diario Granma 13, no. 208 (26 de julio del 2009), www.granma.co.
cu/2009/07/26/nacional/artic27.html.

88. Leon Trotsky, *The Revolution Betrayed* (New York: Merit, 1965), 267.

89. "Interview with Maurice Zeitlin," in Bonachea and Valdés, *Che: Selected Works of Ernesto Guevara*, 392–93.

90. Ibid., 393.

91. Guevara, *Apuntes críticos a la economía política*, 137.

92. For a detailed discussion of "Leninism in power" and its relationship to totalitarian Stalinism, see my book *Before Stalinism: The Rise and Fall of Soviet Democracy*.

93. See, among other sources, Pierre Broué, *The German Revolution, 1917–1923* (Chicago: Haymarket Books, 2006); Pierre Broué, *The Revolution and the Civil War in Spain* (Chicago: Haymarket Books, 2008); Peter Fryer, *Hungarian Tragedy* (London: D. Dobson, 1956); and Colin Barker, *Revolutionary Rehearsals* (Chicago: Haymarket Books, 2008).

Chapter Four

1. Néstor Kohan, "El Che leía a Trotsky: Diálogo con Orlando Borrego, compañero y colaborador del Che en el Ministerio de Industrias," *Cuba Nuestra Digital* (4 de enero del 2008): 3, http://www.cubanuestra.nu/web/article.asp?artID=10547.

2. For an excellent discussion of how the meaning of the term "dictatorship of the proletariat" radically changed from the nineteenth to the twentieth centuries, see Hal Draper, *The "Dictatorship of the Proletariat" from Marx to Lenin* (New York: Monthly Review Press, 1987).

3. Speech of March 25, 1964, to the sixth plenary session of the First Conference for Trade and Development in Geneva. "Exposición de Ernesto Che Guevara ministro de industria y jefe de la delegación de Cuba en la I Conferencia ara el comercio y el desarrollo (Ginebra, 1964)," in Ernesto Che Guevara, *Escritos Económicos*, 129–30 (Córdoba, Argentina: Cuadernos de Pasado y Presente, 1969) and Ernesto Che Guevara "La conferencia para el comercio y desarrollo en Ginebra," n.d., in Ernesto Che Guevara, *Escritos Económicos*, 117–18.

4. For an insightful critique of the "unequal exchange" theory, see chapter 5, "Black Reformism: The Theory of Unequal Exchange," in *Capitalism and Theory*, Michael Kidron (London: Pluto Press, 1974), 95–123. See also Anwar Shaikh, "Foreign Trade and the Law of Value, Part I," *Science and Society* 43, no. 3 (1979): 281–302, and particularly "Foreign Trade and the Law of Value, Part II," *Science and Society* 44, no. 1 (1980): 27–57, especially sections 2 and 3 (41–55) and Summary and Conclusions (55–57). "Dependency theory" enshrined this and related ideas that would remain highly influential in the social sciences for more than a decade.

5. Ernesto Che Guevara, *Apuntes críticos a la economía política*, editado por María del Carmen Ariet García (NP: Ocean Press, 2006), 70. (The book cover does not clarify whether the book was published in Havana or in Australia, where the headquarters of Ocean Press is located.) These *Apuntes* were Guevara's private notes written between 1965 and 1966 after he had resigned from the Cuban government to engage in guerrilla warfare abroad. They were published forty years later, long after the Soviet Union had disappeared.

6. Ibid., 229.

7. Ibid., 209.

8. Speech at the Second Economic Seminar of Afro-Asian Solidarity in Algiers on February 24, 1965, in "Revolution and Underdevelopment," in *Che: Selected Works of Ernesto Guevara,* eds. Rolando E. Bonachea and Nelson P. Valdés (Cambridge, MA: MIT Press, 1969), 351–52.

9. Guevara, *Apuntes críticos a la economía política*, 125.

10. See, for example, Che Guevara's "On the Budgetary System of Finance," published in 1964 where he clearly explains the origin of NEP as necessitated by the prevailing economic situation in Russia. See Bonachea and Valdés, *Che: Selected Works of Ernesto Guevara,* 115–16.

11. Guevara, *Apuntes críticos a la economía política*, 246.

12. Friederich Engels, *Socialism: Utopian and Scientific,* trans. Edward Aveling (New York: Little Marx Library, International Publishers, 1972), 73–75.

13. There are times and places, such as Spain in the 1930s, when movements with highly developed collectivist politics, such as those of anarchist peasants, agricultural workers, and urban artisans in Andalusia and Catalonia, may favor the socialization of small rural and urban productive property.

14. For an important reflection on the thinking and relationship of the Bolsheviks to the peasantry in the Soviet Union of the 1920s, see chapter 1, "The Peasant Question and the Origins of Stalinism: Rethinking the Destruction of the October Revolution," in John Eric Marot, *The October Revolution in Prospect and Retrospect: Interventions in Russian and Soviet History* (Chicago: Haymarket Books, 2013), 11–86.

15. It is not difficult to conceive of many possible kinds of conflict in socialist society. For example, some groups or even political parties might advocate greater consumption today and less saving for the benefit of future generations, while others might advocate exactly the opposite perspective.

16. Guevara, *Apuntes críticos a la economía política*, 185.

17. Ibid., 241.

18. Ibid., 304.

19. Ibid., 294.

20. Ibid., 203.

21. Ibid., 124.

22. Ibid., 183, 301.

23. Ibid., 16.

24. Ibid., 13.

25. Ibid., 214.

26. Of course, hundreds of books and articles have been written about Stalin's policies and his monstrous crimes. See, for example, the Russian socialist's Roy A. Medvedev, *Let History Judge: The Origins and Consequences of Stalinism* (New York: Alfred A. Knopf, 1971). For Stalin's policy toward foreign Communist parties, see Fernando Claudín, *The Communist Movement*, part I: *From Comintern to Cominform* (New York: Monthly Review Press, 1975), and for Stalin's mass killings in Eastern Europe, see Timothy Snyder, *Bloodlands: Europe Between Hitler and Stalin* (New York: Basic Books, 2010).

27. Guevara, *Apuntes críticos a la economía política*, 221.

28. According to Robert M. Bernardo, insofar as firms were supposed to be responsible for their own financial survival under the enterprise self-finance method, it did not work out this way because self-financed firms were bailed out; their deficits were covered by grants or bank loans that were not repaid, and there was no connection between their expenditures and revenues. Robert M. Bernardo, *The Theory of Moral Incentives in Cuba* (University: University of Alabama Press, 1971), 46.

29. There was a fourth but relatively less important debate on the role of banking under socialism. See articles by Luis Alvarez Rom, Marcelo Fernandez Font, and Ernesto Che Guevara in *Man and Socialism in Cuba: The Great Debate*, ed. Bertram Silverman (New York: Atheneum, 1971), 267–316.

30. It is worth noting that the Cuban economist Joaquín Infante, a supporter of the system of enterprise self-finance, specifically invoked the Soviet Union as a model and particularly Nikita S. Khrushchev's promise that within the decade of the 1960s, the gross and per capita product of the Soviet Union would surpass that of the United States. Joaquín Infante, "On the Operation of the Auto-Financed Enterprise," in Silverman, *Man and Socialism in Cuba,* 183.

31. "On the Budgetary System of Finance," in Bonachea and Valdés, *Che: Selected Works of Ernesto Guevara*, 121.

32. Guevara, *Apuntes críticos a la economía política*, 155.

33. Ibid., 281.

34. Helen Yaffe, *Che Guevara: The Economics of Revolution* (London: Palgrave MacMillan, 2009), 204–7.

35. Andrés Vilariño, "Finanzas, dinero y circulación monetaria," *Teoría y Practica* (Febrero 1967): 29–45, as quoted in Carmelo Mesa-Lago, "Ideological, Political, and Economic Factors in the Cuban Controversy on Material Versus Moral Incentives," *Journal of Interamerican Studies and World Affairs* 14 (February 1972): 81–82.

36. Cited in Carmelo Mesa-Lago, *Cuba in the 1970s: Pragmatism and Institu-*

tionalization (Albuquerque: University of New Mexico Press, 1974), 43.

37. Guevara, *Apuntes críticos a la economía política*, 153.

38. Ibid., 275.

39. Karl Marx, "Critique of the Gotha Program," in *The Marx-Engels Reader*, 2nd ed., ed. Robert C. Tucker (New York: W.W. Norton, 1978), 531.

40. Guevara, *Apuntes críticos a la economía política*, 19.

41. Ibid., 120.

42. Ibid., 19.

43. Goran Musić, "Yugoslavia, Workers' Self-Management as State Paradigm," in *Ours to Master and to Win: Workers' Control from the Commune to the Present*, eds. Immanuel Ness and Dario Azzellini (Chicago: Haymarket Books, 2011), 178.

44. Ibid., 179.

45. Saul Estrin, "Yugoslavia: The Case of Self-Managing Market Socialism," *Journal of Economic Perspectives* 5, no. 4 (Fall 1991): 4.

46. Musić, "Yugoslavia, Workers' Self-Management," 181.

47. Mitja Kamusić, "Economic Efficiency and Workers' Self-Management," in *A Reader: Self-Governing Socialism*, vol. 2, *Sociology and Politics: Economics*, eds. Branko Horvat, Mihailo Markovic, and Rusi Supek (White Plains, NY: International Arts and Sciences Press, 1975), 222.

48. Guevara, *Apuntes críticos a la economía política*, 381.

49. Ibid., 422.

50. "Introduction," in Silverman, *Man and Socialism in Cuba: The Great Debate*, 10–11.

51. Bureau of Foreign Commerce, US Department of Commerce, *Investment in Cuba: Basic Information for United States Businessmen* (Washington, DC: Government Printing Office, 1956), 73. These figures probably underestimated the number of small enterprises since it is reasonable to assume that the 21.4 percent of enterprises that did not respond and for which the number of employees was unknown were overwhelmingly small.

52. Alexis Codina, "Experiences of Control Under the Budgetary System," in *Man and Socialism in Cuba*, ed. Silverman, 206–8.

53. Ibid., 210–14.

54. Carmelo Mesa-Lago, *The Economy of Socialist Cuba: A Two-Decade Appraisal* (Albuquerque: University of New Mexico Press, 1981), 16.

55. Joaquin Infante, "On the Operation of the Auto-Financed Enterprise," in *Man and Socialism in Cuba*, ed. Silverman, 183.

56. Archibald R. M. Ritter, *The Economic Development of Revolutionary Cuba: Strategy and Performance* (New York: Praeger, 1974), 150–53.

57. Carmelo Mesa-Lago, *Market, Socialist and Mixed Economies, Comparative Policy and Performance: Chile, Cuba and Costa Rica* (Baltimore: Johns Hopkins University Press, 2000), 219–20.

58. Bernardo, *The Theory of Moral Incentives in Cuba*, 112.

59. János Kornai described the most common form of this system as "self-supporting—assisted." Under this form the firm is a unit with "independent accounting." It must cover its expenses from its own revenue, but if the firm gets into trouble, it will typically negotiate with the state some form of financial support. János Kornai, *Economics of Shortage*, vol. B (Amsterdam: North-Holland, 1980), 564.

60. Introduction to Silverman, *Man and Socialism in Cuba*, 10.

61. Luis Martínez-Fernández, *Revolutionary Cuba: A History* (Gainesville: University Press of Florida, 2014), 131.

62. Ibid., 132.

63. Mesa-Lago, *Market, Socialist and Mixed Economies*, 232–33.

64. Ibid., 233.

65. For a more extensive treatment of the problems and contradictions of the Cuban economy, see chapter 2, "Economic Development and the Standard of Living Since the 1959 Revolution," of my book *Cuba Since the Revolution of 1959: A Critical Assessment* (Chicago: Haymarket Books, 2011), 51–95. Janos Kornai's *Economics of Shortage* (New York: Elsevier, 1980) explores in depth issues such as the tendency of managers to accumulate resources beyond their production needs, which is essential to an understanding of the problems and contradictions of Soviet-type economies.

66. Guevara, "On the Budgetary System of Finance," in Bonachea and Valdés, *Che: Selected Works of Ernesto Guevara*, 128. This definition assumed the nationalization of private property and rule of the vanguard Communist Party that Guevara continued to see as essential to socialism.

67. Ernest Mandel, *Late Capitalism* (London: Verso, 1978), 594.

68. I want to thank Mel Bienenfeld for his help in clarifying the issues discussed in this section. Personal communication of July 23, 2014.

69. Guevara, "On the Budgetary System of Finance," in Bonachea and Valdés, *Che: Selected Works of Ernesto Guevara*, 127–28.

70. Ibid., and Guevara, *Apuntes críticos a la economía política*, 156.

71. For this and other relevant features of the 1965 economic reforms in the USSR, see Alec Nove, *An Economic History of the U.S.S.R.*, new ed. (London: Penguin Books, 1990), 367–68.

72. Guevara, *Apuntes críticos a la economía política*, 429.

73. Alberto Mora committed suicide in September 1972. In 1971, he supported the persecuted poet Heberto Padilla and was briefly detained by the government. Alejandro Armengol, "La decencia tiene dos nombres," *Cubaencuentro*, March 10, 2006, http://cubaencuentro.com/opinion/articulos/la-decencia-tiene-dos-nombres-13451.

74. Alberto Mora, "On the Operation of the Law of Value in the Cuban Economy," in *Man and Socialism in Cuba: The Great Debate*, Silverman, 219–30.

75. Some foreigners such as Charles Bettelheim and Ernest Mandel also participated in the "great debate" on both sides of the issues at stake but took for granted and failed to criticize the undemocratic structures of the one-party state underlying the high-level controversy. See Charles Bettelheim, "On Socialist Planning and the Level of the Development of the Productive Forces," and Ernest Mandel, "Mercantile Categories in the Period of Transition," in *Man and Socialism in Cuba: The Great Debate*, Silverman, 31–59 and 60–97, respectively.

76. Guevara, *Apuntes críticos a la economía política*, 202.

77. Ibid., 146–47.

78. Ibid., 202.

79. Néstor Kohan, "Diálogo con Orlando Borrego, compañero y colaborador del Che en el Ministerio de Industrias: Che Guevara, lector de El Capital," *Rebelión*, July 2, 2003, http://www.rebelion.org/noticia.php?id=51.

80. Hal Draper, "The Two Souls of Socialism," in *Socialism from Below*, ed. E. Haberkern (Atlantic Highlands, NJ: Humanities Press, 1992), 21, and Arthur Lipow, *Authoritarian Socialism in America: Edward Bellamy and the Nationalist Movement* (Berkeley and Los Angeles: University of California Press, 1982), 26.

81. Mesa-Lago, *Market, Socialist and Mixed Economies*, 218.

82. Samuel Farber, "Material and Non-Material Work Incentives as Ideologies and Practices of Order," *Review of Radical Political Economics* 14, no. 4 (Winter 1982): 33.

83. Contrary to a widespread perception, the policy of material incentives has not necessarily been more economically or politically liberal from a popular and working-class perspective. It can, as in the extreme case of Stalin's Russia, sharply increase industrial speed, unpaid overtime, deteriorating working conditions, and rivalry among workers.

84. Mesa-Lago, *Market, Socialist and Mixed Economies*, 211–12.

85. Marifeli Pérez-Stable, *The Cuban Revolution: Origins, Course and Legacy*, 2nd ed. (New York: Oxford University Press, 1999), 156.

86. Mesa-Lago, *Market, Socialist and Mixed Economies*, 276.

87. Pérez-Stable, *The Cuban Revolution*, 281.

88. Alexander Eckstein, *China's Economic Development: The Interplay of Scarcity and Ideology* (Ann Arbor: University of Michigan Press, 1975), 333; see also Charles Hoffmann, *Work Incentive Practices and Policies in the People's Republic of China, 1953–1965* (Albany: State University of New York Press, 1967), 124.

89. See, for example, the report of a *New York Times* journalist about the use of the terms "right" and "left" in Mao's home province of Hunan. Edward A. Gargan, "Mao's Home Province Proves Stubborn," *New York Times*, May 26, 1987.

90. I want to thank Charles Post for his help in formulating this point.

Conclusion

1. For a detailed historical analysis of the role of the old pro-Moscow Communist Party in the early revolutionary period, see my article "The Cuban Communists in the Early Stages of the Cuban Revolution: Revolutionaries or Reformists?" *Latin American Research Review* 13, no. 1 (1983): 59–83, and chapter five, "The Role of the Soviet Union and the Cuban Communists," in my book *The Origins of the Cuban Revolution Reconsidered* (Chapel Hill: University of North Carolina Press, 2006).

2. Camilo Cienfuegos was the fourth important leader of the Cuban Revolution; he disappeared in October 1959 while flying in a small plane. Neither the plane nor his body were ever found.

3. For an analysis of Raúl Castro's contemporary reform program and how it relates to his political record in the early years of the Cuban Revolution, see my article *"Raúl's Cuba"* in *Boston Review*, September/October 2013, http://www.bostonreview.net/world/cuba-raul-castro-reform-democracy.

4. Of course, this does not mean that the politics of Guevara and the Castro brothers were immune to working-class and popular pressures in the sense of having to satisfy, at least to a degree, mass aspirations and expectations. But that is by no means the same thing as the establishment of democratic institutional mechanisms holding the leaders responsible to the people, including the right of the people to remove their leaders.

5. Meeting of the Ministry of Industry on February 22, 1964, as reported in Ernesto Che Guevara, *Apuntes críticos a la economía política*, ed. María del Carmen Ariet (Centro de Estudios Che Guevara and Ocean Press, 2006), 303–4.

6. Liberal and conservative critics of Marxism have claimed that Marx and Engels's proclamation of the "dictatorship of the proletariat" gave the lie to their democratic pretensions. There are many problems with this point of view, including the fact that in Marx and Engels's time the term "dictatorship" had a very different meaning than it acquired in the twentieth century, especially after Stalin's rule in the Soviet Union. For a thorough discussion of this question, see Hal Draper, *The "Dictatorship of the Proletariat" from Marx to Lenin* (New York: Monthly Review Press, 1987).

7. Ernesto Guevara, *Socialism and Man in Cuba*, in *Che: Selected Works of Ernesto Guevara,* eds. Rolando E. Bonachea and Nelson P. Valdés (Cambridge, MA: MIT Press, 1969), 162–63, 169.

8. Max Weber, *The Protestant Ethic and the Spirit of Capitalism*, trans. Talcott Parsons (Los Angeles: Roxbury, 1996), 181–82.

Index

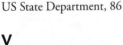

About Haymarket Books

Haymarket Books is a nonprofit, progressive book distributor and publisher, a project of the Center for Economic Research and Social Change. We believe that activists need to take ideas, history, and politics into the many struggles for social justice today. Learning the lessons of past victories, as well as defeats, can arm a new generation of fighters for a better world. As Karl Marx said, "The philosophers have merely interpreted the world; the point, however, is to change it."

We take inspiration and courage from our namesakes, the Haymarket Martyrs, who gave their lives fighting for a better world. Their 1886 struggle for the eight-hour day reminds workers around the world that ordinary people can organize and struggle for their own liberation.

For more information and to shop our complete catalog of titles, visit us online at www.haymarketbooks.org.

Also Available from Haymarket Books

Brazil's Dance with the Devil: The World Cup, the Olympics, and the Struggle for Democracy
Dave Zirin

Cuba Since the Revolution of 1959: A Critical Assessment
Samuel Farber

The Dispossessed: Chronicles of the Desterrados of Colombia
Alfredo Molano, Foreword by Aviva Chomsky

From Rebellion to Reform in Bolivia: Class Struggle, Indigenous Liberation, and the Politics of Evo Morales
Jeffery R. Webber

The Mexican Revolution: A Short History 1910–1920
Stuart Easterling

Rogue States: The Rule of Force in World Affairs
Noam Chomsky

Year 501: The Conquest Continues
Noam Chomsky

About the Author

Samuel Farber was born and raised in Marianao, Cuba, and came to the United States in February 1958. He earned a PhD in sociology from the University of California at Berkeley in 1969 and taught at a number of colleges and universities, including UCLA and, most recently, Brooklyn College of the City University of New York, where he is a professor emeritus of political science. His scholarship on Cuba is extensive and includes many articles and two previous books: *Revolution and Reaction in Cuba, 1933–1960* (Wesleyan University Press, 1976) and *The Origins of the Cuban Revolution Reconsidered* (University of North Carolina Press, 2006). He is also the author of *Before Stalinism: The Rise and Fall of Soviet Democracy* (Polity/Verso, 1990) and *Social Decay and Transformation: A View from the Left* (Lexington Books, 2000). Farber was active in the Cuban high school student movement against Fulgencio Batista in the 1950s and has been involved in socialist politics for more than fifty years.